URGENT CALLS

FROM

DISTANT PLACES

URGENT CALLS FROM DISTANT PLACES

AN EMERGENCY DOCTOR'S NOTES ABOUT LIFE AND DEATH ON THE FRONTIERS OF EAST AFRICA

Marc-David Munk, MD

Published in the United States by Creemore Press.
Creemore and the Creemore logomark are registered trademarks.

Book design and typesetting by CoverKitchen
Cartography by Elbie Bentley
Publisher's Cataloging-in-Publication Data
provided by Five Rainbows Cataloging Services
Names: Munk, Marc-David, 1973- author.
Title: Urgent calls from distant places : an emergency doctor's notes about life and death on the frontiers of East Africa / Marc-David Munk, MD.
Description: Boston, MA : Creemore Press, 2024. | Also available in audiobook format.
Identifiers: LCCN 2023921105 (print) | ISBN 979-8-9894724-0-6 (hardcover) | ISBN 979-8-9894724-2-0 (paperback) | ISBN 979-8-9894724-1-3 (Kindle ebook) | ISBN 979-8-9894724-3-7 (EPUB)
Subjects: LCSH: Physicians--Biography. | African Medical and Research Foundation. | Emergency medical services. | Airplane ambulances. | Primary health care--Africa, East. | Autobiography. | BISAC: BIOGRAPHY & AUTOBIOGRAPHY / Medical (incl. Patients) | MEDICAL / Essays. | TRAVEL / Africa / East / General. | TRAVEL / Essays & Travelogues.
Classification: LCC RA996.55.K4 M86 2024 (print) | LCC RA996.55.K4 (ebook) | DDC 610/.92--dc23.
Maps Derived from the following sources, under permissible use:
-Natural Earth: Cultural and Physical Features
-OpenStreetMap: Coastlines under CC BY-SA 2.0 license.
https://www.openstreetmap.org/copyright
-GHS Urban Centre Database: Global Human Settlement Layer (GHS-UCDB) GHS Urban Centre Database 2015

To Oscar and Nora.

It's a once-in-a-century "plastic moment"
when everything shifts.
May you become the worldly, curious,
and ethical leaders the world needs.

To Martina,
who knows my inner places
and gracefully accepts my lonesome plans.

And to Linda,
who would have been proud.

CONTENTS

AUTHOR'S NOTE

It is impossible to truly understand a place without being part of its fabric. I believe this, and I know it to be true. I was *not* a part of the fabric of Africa; I was a short-term visitor, an emergency physician who spent several months as a "flying doctor" caring for patients. But Africa changed me. It got under my skin. My time there forced me to confront profound moral questions about modernity, geopolitics, colonialism, and the rationing of medicine—questions that we in the West only rarely engage with. The experiences I had in Africa offered profound opportunities for reflection on some of the deeper questions one confronts over the course of a thoughtful life: *What purpose do I serve as a man? As a doctor? What purpose* should *I serve? In a continent where millions are suffering, were my efforts and my team's resources, which were marshalled to save one person at a time, worthy? Are developed countries able to play the long game in foreign policy? Are humans equipped to comprehend the decades-later consequences of their polices? Do they even care?*

Over the course of writing this book, I had to stretch into uncomfortable positions. Though even scholars struggle to distill centuries of African history into a coherent narrative, that is what I have made every effort to do in this book. To understand—or even to glimpse briefly—the state of nations of Africa, one must wrap oneself in context. I am not a historian, however; any mistakes made here are my own.

Despite my academic ignorance of the continent's deep history, despite my limited time there and the limited friendships I made, and despite my own very different roots, I nevertheless felt compelled to write this book. In doing so, I realized that, though I was only a short-term visitor, Africa had become part of the fabric of *my* life. And my fresh eyes might serve as a bridge to readers in more developed parts of the world.

Some housekeeping details: It also goes without saying that the conclusions and observations in this book are mine alone and do not necessarily reflect those of the air ambulance service I flew with, AMREF Flying Doctors, whose sole purpose is providing health care to people in Africa. To protect the privacy of my patients and colleagues, I have changed the names and identifying characteristics of the people in this book. Finally, the stories in this book were collected over a period of five years and took another decade to put on paper. I relied on my memory and on the notes I took and blog entries I wrote years earlier. Colleagues may remember certain details differently; such are the challenges of time. Despite these limitations, the missions I describe are real. Each rescue happened.

I have written this book to shine a light on the continent, and on medicine, so that others might explore the questions I confronted. I hope that they might find their way to new answers, and perhaps to a new way of thinking—about Africa, about respectful coexistence with strangers, and about a doctor's responsibilities to the world.

Marc-David Munk
Nairobi
September 2023

Body and soul contain a thousand possibilities out of which you can build many 'I's. But in only one of them is there a congruence of the elector and the elected. Only one—which you will never find until you have excluded all those superficial and fleeting possibilities of being and doing with which you toy, out of curiosity or wonder or greed, and which hinder you from casting anchor in the experience of the mystery of life, and the consciousness of the talent entrusted to you which is your I.

— Dag Hammarskjöld, *Markings*

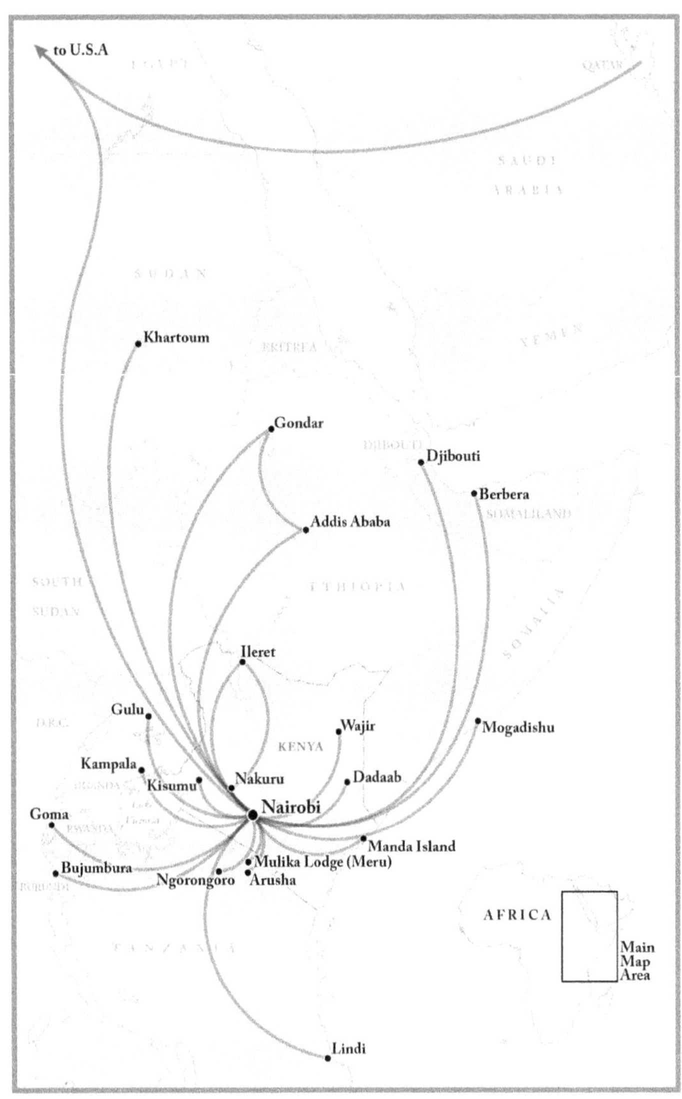

Medical Evacuation Flights, 2008/ 2012

INTRODUCTION

The airliner was filled with a mix of African businessmen in shiny suits; worn-out UN workers in khakis and Oxford cloth shirts; evangelicals, who had prayed in a huddle and held hands before boarding; excited National Health Service nurses, home for a visit; and a gaggle of Germans in sensible shoes whom I guessed were headed for safari.

We had crossed the Kenyan frontier in darkness and begun the descent toward Nairobi's Kenyatta airport. Only when the city lights appeared in the distance did I suddenly feel ill at ease, uncharacteristically anxious about this trip.

The flight attendants made their rounds, collecting drinks and checking seatbelts. I checked that my elastic polyester document pouch was still strapped to my abdomen. In it was a passport, a few hundred US dollars, and a copy of my newly issued Kenyan medical license to show the authorities. I'd also brought a medium-sized canvas duffel bag that held enough clothes to last for a month—nothing fancy—plus some granola bars, mosquito repellent, and a pair of sturdy shoes. In a backpack, I carried my small laptop, mainly to Skype and write a blog for friends. I'd told them I would regularly share my adventures doing medical evacuation work in East Africa over the next month.

In an email to me, just before I left the US a day earlier, the coordinators at the AMREF Flying Doctors Service in Nairobi wrote that they were delighted that I would join them as a volunteer doctor. Get some rest, they had warned, because I'd be busy with my orientation sessions to the air ambulances and to the medical equipment in the morning. An emergency flight was always a possibility.

I had never been to Africa, but I had worked in resource-poor settings before. I reminded myself that I was a solid emergency physician with good judgment. Also, I had exactly the right education needed to work abroad. I had staffed American air ambulances for years, and Flying Doctors had a great reputation.

Sitting in that plane, waiting for our final descent, my concerns were less of a practical nature and more existential. What was I doing so far from home? Why was I voluntarily assuming the significant risks of staffing medevac flights in most-remote Africa? What did I hope to discover?

I was working on the answers. In moments of clarity, I felt that, somehow, I was where I needed to be. I wanted to clear my head and figure out what was to come next in a career that had left me in a dip, disillusioned with organized medicine at a young age.

I had no illusions that I would make a meaningful dent in Africa's health care problems. I was one person, new to the continent, there for a short time. Selfishly, I just wanted to get back to the fundamentals of being a good doctor by providing care to patients who desperately needed me, one at a time. Simple enough.

The pilots circled Nairobi and prepared to land. In a few hours, I would begin a month on-duty as a flying doctor, responding to calls for emergency medical help from a dozen countries in East Africa. I had no idea what lay ahead. I hoped that I would find what I was looking for.

SECTION 1: DRY SEASON, 2008

I sought trains; I found passengers.

— Paul Theroux

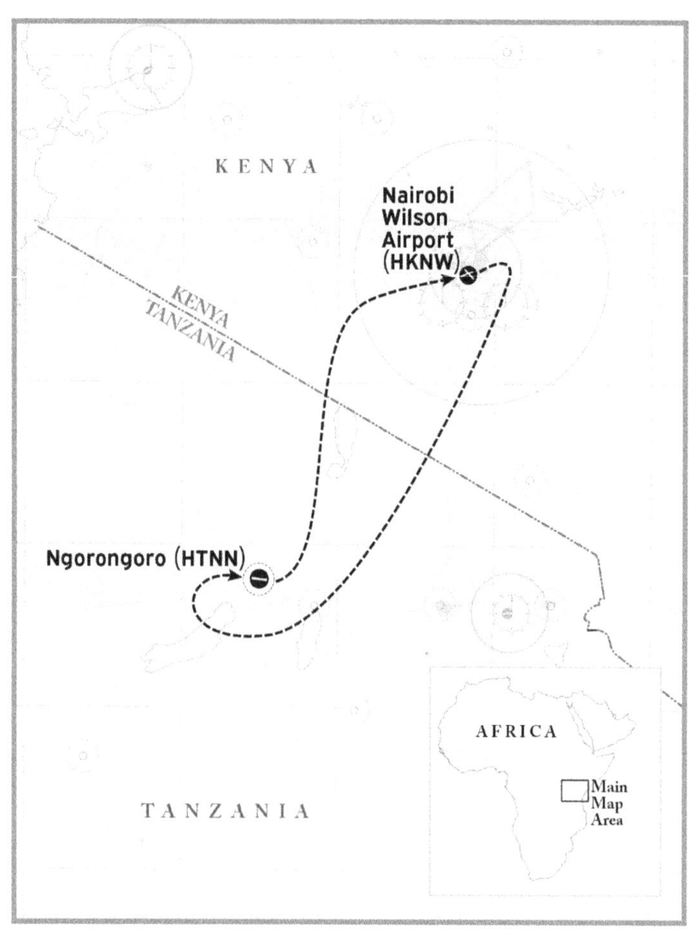

Evacuation from Ngorongoro, Tanzania, using a King Air

LITTLE BOY

We began every morning at that same hour, using what we were pleased to call the Nairobi Aerodrome, climbing away from it with derisive clamour, while the burghers of the town twitched in their beds and dreamed perhaps of all unpleasant things that drone — of wings and stings, and corridors in Bedlam.

— Beryl Markham

Nairobi was hot and chaotic and had myriad types of petty crime. Navigating the city required alertness. Most of the time, I was cocooned in the passenger seat of a Flying Doctors' ambulance. The drivers took an almost matronly interest in my well-being, reminding me to keep the windows rolled up and the doors locked. It was 2008, an unsettled time in Kenya; a few months earlier, there had been riots following a contested election. Deep tribal resentments, worsened by a long tradition of graft, set off a wave of ethnic killings and had shut down tourism. The UN Secretary General had to intervene and establish a power-sharing government. The entire country was walking on eggshells.

Due to its massive population squeezed into a city designed for far fewer people, Nairobi was continually frenetic. At all hours, the streets were packed with cars and bikes and matatu, the shared vans whose destinations were painted brightly on their sides. All of us drove bumper-to-bumper past children in the median selling bottles of water which had been purchased in the distant past from a shop and since refilled from the tap, then cleverly re-sealed. Drinking it was certain to result in intense diarrhea. Every inch of the city was occupied; there were rusting sedans up on bricks in front of makeshift car repair shops and popup tarpaulins laid out on the concrete, displaying secondhand clothes, cheap Chinese extension cords, electric kettles, and phone chargers. Everyone carried parcels, cube-like bundles of stuff wrapped with plastic and string, and groceries. The city hummed.

The Flying Doctors logo on the door of the ambulance and on my uniform jacket seemed to provide a halo of protection from the hawkers. Everyone in Nairobi knew what the Flying Doctors did, and they appeared to take pride in what had become a hometown success story. But even without the uniform, I was rarely, if ever, hassled. Most Kenyans were gentle and decent; some were noticeably formal—perhaps a consequence of the schools, which offered a strict British public-school approach to education. Good humor and warmth, however, seemed to be a national trait. It was easy to feel welcome.

This umbrella of goodwill began on my very first day in Africa, when Pato, one of Flying Doctors' full-time drivers, met me in the hectic baggage claim at the Nairobi airport with a sign. Pato had left his ambulance double parked outside the International Arrivals doors, its blinkers flashing. He seemed exempt from the attentions of the otherwise fastidious parking officers. Throwing my duffel bag into the back of the vehicle, next to the stretcher, I jumped in the front, and we managed to escape the gauntlet of hawkers and ersatz taxi drivers and drove into the city.

Pato was a slight but serious fellow of about thirty years old. He was one of the best ambulance drivers I've ever met. He wiggled the vehicle through gaps in traffic and snarled roundabouts, and he seemed to work all hours without complaint. On this first ride, we were headed from Nairobi's international airport to its smaller regional airport, called Wilson Airport. Wilson was the Flying Doctors' base and the site of Kenya's Aero Club, which would be my home for the next month.

After central Nairobi's extreme energy, it was a relief to enter the gated airport grounds and drive past the guard shack to the Aero Club. Home was to be a simple bungalow, which contained a hard bed, a mosquito net, and a TV that offered only local Kenyan channels—mostly soap operas, local news, and excessively loud ads from local shops. The club was comfortable enough, but it was an anachronism, a dusty legacy of times past when white Africans would fly into the city for weekends from their rural farms and estates. The club had a long bar, a dining room, and a few rooms available for rent. On Fridays, the place would fill up and the garden would burst with noise. But most nights were silent and empty.

I quickly established a routine. Flying Doctors provided a bicycle, and I would bike the mile between the Aero Club and the Flying Doctors' hangar using the protected service road inside the airport. The bike was an old-fashioned single-gear unit, and I felt daintily Victorian heading back and forth in my uniform shirt and work boots. I would head to the base in the mornings. Usually, there would be a mission being organized or a range of administrative tasks to be done at the hangar: equipment checks, medication reviews, and paperwork.

My first rescue came soon enough: on my first morning in Africa, we were headed to Tanzania. I had a short time to get ready.

I first saw them waiting for the planes at the edge of the dirt runway in Tanzania. There were seven people, five of them children; all were injured to various degrees, but from a distance it looked like the kids were all moving. Except one. On the grassy earth, unconscious, lay one little boy.

Slowly, the story came together for me. There had been a celebration in Tanzania, just across the Kenyan border, the night before. Not far. The family had dressed up in their nice clothes, excited for a night out, and driven several hours to the party. They had eaten well and laughed with friends. When it got late, the mom and dad belatedly said goodbye to their hosts and carried their tired kids to the car. On the way home to Kenya, the children quickly fell asleep—like any kids would—lulled by the sound of the car engine. The night sky was pitch-black; it is unlikely that the car's headlights were able to fully pierce the dark. The mom and dad opened a window to the fresh night air and kept the radio low, to avoid waking the kids.

Without warning, disaster struck. In a blind instant, the SUV hit—at full speed, and without braking—the back of an unlit tractor wending down the dark roadway.

The children's mother later told me that after the explosion of noise and airbags and broken glass, there was only lingering smoke and a profound silence. Then, in the back of the vehicle, the children began to scream. The adults, seated in the front, were most damaged; they had broken their arms, their legs, their backs, and their pelvises. Protected in the back, the children had fared better and been left bruised and pummeled, but not seriously injured.

Except there was one child who hadn't been in the back. He was a little boy who had been sleeping in his mother's arms. The mother didn't remember the air-bag. She said that, upon impact, the little boy had been launched from her arms into the windshield. When the dust settled, there was a crater in the glass. The little boy, sprawled on top of the dashboard, was unconscious.

What happened next was ugly. The noise of the crash had roused the locals, mostly subsistence farmers. Despite the dark and the lateness of the hour, people emerged from nearby huts and shanties and began milling around the car. Some tried to help; others only watched. While the stunned family crawled out of the wreckage through one of the SUV's doors, thieves entered through the broken windows. They helped themselves to bags, phones, wallets, and everything else of value.

One good soul called the local tiny hospital for an ambulance. And, knowing that their wounds were severe, the injured husband managed to dial Flying Doctors in Nairobi directly, using a borrowed phone.

Hours passed as they waited for the clinic's ambulance. When it arrived, the family —the wounded parents, the unconscious little boy, the panicked children—were taken to the small rural hospital nearby and were told that they must wait for treatment until morning. The doctors at the hospital couldn't do much, and Flying Doctors wouldn't fly until dawn.

Notified of the mission early that morning by the control center, I sat in a taxi that had idled in the dark outside the Aero Club as I finished my shower and found a uniform shirt, my boots, my crew ID badge, and my stethoscope. The hangar was busy. The flight coordinators had decided to send two planes for the seven patients, and the crew were busy stocking both planes. Nurse Michael and I would go on one King Air, and nurses Asher and Kione would take the other. The team moved with lightning efficiency; maybe twenty minutes had elapsed between my alarm clock and wheels-up.

Once in the air, the second plane stayed not far off our wing for most of the flight. Dawn arrived as we crossed into Tanzanian airspace, and I could see the rural homes awakening, movement in the fields, smoke starting to rise from cooking fires. Descending toward the crude runway cut into the savannah, the pilots of our plane circled several times to make sure the field was free of livestock and wild animals before lining up for a landing. We flew just above the trees, then lowered quickly into a clearing, which was really nothing more than a length of red earth scratched into the grass. We landed with a bump, decelerated quickly, and taxied over the rough ground to the far end of the strip. The pilots made a sharp turn, pointing our nose back toward the strip, and we hugged the edges of the field to give the next plane room to land.

The King Air is a big twin turboprop. Its wingspan is almost sixty feet. With its bright spotlights on, the second plane approached the strip at an angle to compensate for side winds. On its wings, warning lights alternated, right and left, flashes of bright white. Despite the plane's width and speed, the pilots descended with total confidence above the trees and touched down without incident at the nearest edge of the field.

It's hard to convey the immense power of that moment. I was struck by the sheer improbability of landing a massive turboprop like the King Air on such a small strip of grass, the confidence of the pilots, the absolute stability of the descent, and the plain competence of the entire operation. I was strangely moved by this moment of grace. The emotional detachment I carried on missions faded for a brief moment; I was simply awed by the awesome execution.

Once Kione and Asher's plane pulled next to ours, it was time to work. After the pilots shut down the engines, we grabbed the equipment bags, and the four of us approached the muddy road next to the strip where two ambulances from the hospital had been waiting for us. As we got close, I could see several bandaged bodies lying on the grass next to the white vehicles; there were others sitting up next to them. When we got to the ambulances, we immediately opened the rear doors; inside, there were stretchers with more bodies on them.

They teach us that our priority, when walking into this sort of situation, is to make order from chaos. You need to quantify what the situation is: you must sort the injured into groups, prioritize the care each patient needs, and then—finally—make a plan for how to deal with the injured in relation to the greatest needs and the available resources.

There were seven patients. Our priority quickly became triage; we needed to figure out who was hurt and how badly. The protocols meant that those without a pulse (called "black") would receive no care; critically ill ("red") patients would become immediate priorities, followed by the moderately ill ("yellow"); and then the "walking wounded" ("green") would be treated. We had one red, two yellow, and four green patients. Kione and Asher would manage six patients: they would start IVs, splint bones, immobilize necks, and bandage bleeding wounds. Michael and I would manage the sole "red" patient: the two-year-old boy who had been launched into the windshield and was now minutes from death.

He was a beautiful, strong little boy. He wore a

stained diaper but no shirt or shoes, and he was covered in dirt and glass dust. The hospital hadn't had the resources or experience to provide any care, so the ambulance attendants had simply laid him on a bare stretcher, on his back, in one of the ambulances.

We always begin with an assessment of three things: airway, breathing, and circulation. Can the child maintain a patent airway? Is he breathing on his own, or does he need support? Is his heart pumping blood to his other organs? And can he maintain an acceptable blood pressure? Once those things are assessed as stable, we do a systemic but brief head-to-toe exam to look for injuries. Then we formulate a plan. We are rigid about approaching severe injuries in the same way every time; otherwise, it's too easy to be distracted by, say, a gruesome broken bone and neglect the truly life-threatening airway problem. For emergency doctors, this way of doing things is reflexive—like breathing.

Michael and I didn't like what we were seeing. The boy was unconscious, not crying at all, and there was a trickle of dried blood that ran from his mouth to his ear. He was maintaining an airway, barely, and was working hard to breathe. With concern, we watched him struggle to take frequent, shallow breaths. He had bruises on his head and his abdomen, which was puffed out and firm. This was a serious injury.

We slid an immobilization device under the child. Michael picked up both and, holding them as flat as possible, delicately carried the boy to the plane. Once he was on our stretcher, we connected the monitor and checked the boy's vital signs. The numbers weren't good; they supported our initial impressions of shock and respiratory failure.

There was a lot that needed to be done immediately, but our priority was to support the boy's breathing and protect his airway. We had to keep him from choking on blood and vomit. We also had to ensure sure that he was perfusing his organs with oxygenated blood. Michael bent down and started two tiny IVs in the boy's fragile arm veins.

There is nothing worse than having to resuscitate a child. Kids are built solidly; their heart and lungs are powerful. Their bones flex; they're not brittle like an old person's. Their bodies resist injury. When children are seriously sick or injured, they hold on for the longest time, until they can't, and then they crash. Adults tend to wither, incrementally and visibly; with them, you have time to prepare for what's next. Not so with children.

Injured kids run against the natural order of things. Their innocence and their vulnerability impose a huge responsibility on a doctor. We must do more than our best; our work must be flawless because the stakes are so high. For most emergency physicians, pediatric resuscitations are rare. We know how to do them, of course, and have practiced again and again. But they are uncommon, and each resuscitation we conduct occupies a permanent place in our heads and is relied upon to guide the next resuscitation.

Fixing kids doesn't come automatically; we don't retain that muscle memory. Because we do pediatric resuscitations infrequently, every step requires concentration and deliberate thought, and we become unavoidably emotionally involved. To counter this, we use checklists and easily remembered color-coded charts to make thinking as effortless as possible. Even pediatric emergency doctors, who see kids all day, infrequently deal with crashing children. That's a blessing.

With the plane's doors open, I rooted through our uncommonly used pediatric airway bag and prepared the equipment for an intubation. We needed to put in a breathing tube and place the child on a ventilator. We unrolled a color-coded measuring tape and, based on his estimated weight, I selected a tiny laryngoscope and an even smaller endotracheal tube. Michael prepared the transport ventilator and placed an oxygen facemask on the little boy, running it on full to allow his body to build up as much of an oxygen reserve as possible.

Next came the complex drug calculations: such a small child required a fraction of the adult dose—and often different medications, as well. I wrote down the calculated doses on an IV bag wrapper, and Michael checked the concentrations in the medication vials and double checked the volume of fluid he had drawn up.

We were precise, so careful. Intubating a child is a fraught procedure with little room for error. Every detail differs from adults—the shape of the airway, the floppiness of the pharynx, the way the head needs to be tilted just so to maintain patency. When all was in place, we did one final check of our equipment to make sure the light on the laryngoscope was bright and the tube was the right size and had been lubricated. Finally, we were ready to go.

To insert a breathing tube in a patient who still has a gag reflex and is breathing, doctors need to follow a discrete sequence. First, we give the patient a strong sedative, an anesthetic. Then we administer a paralyzing drug, which allows for an easier intubation and allows the ventilator to take over breathing completely. Once the drugs have taken effect, we can look into the throat and pass the breathing tube safely. We do things methodically and consistently.

Michael first pushed a strong sedative and then a paralyzing drug into the boy's IV. After a moment, the baby twitched, and then his strained breathing stopped. I inserted the laryngoscope—basically a handle with a blade of steel—into the boy's flaccid mouth. I looked for his vocal cords but could see only saliva. Michael and I began to suction aggressively, using the battery-operated machine, and soon blood and saliva filled the clear suction tubing. Within seconds, the alarm on our monitor started to go off: the boy's oxygen saturation was falling. I had expected this to happen. The little boy, who already was so hurt and compromised, didn't have the lung reserve to go more than a few seconds without breathing, and he had quickly run out of oxygen.

I put down the laryngoscope and placed a pediatric bag-valve mask directly over the boy's mouth, the usual way we get oxygen levels back up to the point where another attempt at intubation would be safe. I began to squeeze the pediatric-sized bag, to push air into the lungs.

But when I looked at his chest, I realized that nothing was happening. I was squeezing the bag, but no air seemed to be entering the boy's lungs. The pulse oximeter began to fall further. There was still no chest rise.

"Bag, Michael," I yelled, as I cupped the facemask with two hands to make a better seal. Michael squeezed the bag aggressively, but nothing was happening; air wasn't moving into the lungs. I could hear the heart-rate monitor beeps coming slower and slower, a truly ominous sign. The little boy was approaching cardiac arrest. I was confused. Why was the air not entering his lungs? Only seconds had passed, but they were dire. What was wrong? I felt a familiar sick feeling in my stomach—the one I get when things spin out of control. Now, I'm truly frightened. This was the worst possible situation. Was there an airway obstruction? Did I need to insert a high-pressure needle jet into his trachea to push air below the obstruction? The situation was unravelling fast.

I thought of blowing into the facemask, mouth to mask. For a second, I stared at Michael. He stared back at me. Then I gasped: "A bag, get me another bag. Michael, get another bag, any bag."

Michael reached into the adult airway bag and

grabbed an adult sized BVM, which was way too large for this child. Without an alternative, I popped the kid's facemask onto the adult bag and squeezed the large bag delicately, with two fingers. I was trying to deliver small volumes of air; too much could cause serious lung trauma.

Michael and I waited. We each held our breaths. At first, there was nothing. And then it happened. His small chest rose. It was working. It was the bag—the bag was the problem. We were now able to push the desperately needed oxygen into his lungs. The monitor started to beep more rapidly, the pulse oximeter climbed, and, within a minute, we were fine. Praise the heavens. Minutes later, I was able to pass a tube, which slid easily between the boy's vocal cords into his trachea, and then we connected him to our ventilator.

The pediatric bag, it turned out, had a defective valve. Perhaps it was a manufacturing error, or maybe it had been assembled incorrectly after cleaning. Either way, we hadn't caught it in our routine equipment checks.

We now had a good airway. We started an IV drip of sedatives and added a long-lasting paralytic to get us through the long plane trip to Nairobi. We closely watched the monitor to follow his end-tidal CO2 and oxygen levels. We placed a foley catheter, gave fluid and medications, and gave antibiotics for the fever he was running—which, given his firm abdomen, we suspected was due to intestinal trauma and peritonitis.

That kind of situation ages you. Fast. To hold a child's life in my hands, manage a rare procedure, plus troubleshoot a strange complication at a critical time required all my mental energies. I was physically exhausted.

With the little boy stabilized, we gave the OK to load the aircraft. Michael and I would take the little boy and his three sisters, and the other flight would carry the adults and the remaining child. We made sure our equipment was loaded and secured, and then the pilots taxied to the end of the grass strip. The planes, one at a time, accelerated at full speed and cleared the trees at the end of the runway before banking sharply and gaining altitude. Once we were in the air, I looked around the plane at the sedated boy and his three older sisters. The girls were mostly unhurt and were happily sucking mints and drinking lemonade, paying rapt attention to Michael and me as we kept their little brother stabilized. I thought about the tenuousness of life and how often we can be blind to that fragility, especially in our own families. By all accounts, the SUV had been destroyed. The odds of seven people surviving such a crash were long.

When we landed, we could see that the entire Flying Doctors' fleet of five ground ambulances had been mobilized, along with extra nurses who had been on desk duty in the control room. I watched through the plane's window, mesmerized by the ambulance's emergency lights which lit the tarmac like a discotheque. With care and no little amount of relief, we carried the patients to the ambulances, climbed aboard, and began a convoy to Kenyatta Hospital, through the busy streets of Nairobi.

When we arrived, we entered the hospital through its dark concrete entranceway and transferred all seven patients to the hospital staff, who were waiting for us in the ED resuscitation rooms. There was a flurry of activity in the resuscitation room where the little boy lay. The nurses in white uniforms leaned over the stretcher, their white caps hair-clipped securely, as they checked his IV lines. Surgeons hovered and pushed on the boy's abdomen and made a decision to bring him to the operating room immediately.

This was our moment of transition. Our work was done; we had gotten our patients to the hospital safely and then relinquished them to the next team. This was a simple matter of process; it was what Flying Doctors did. But still, it was hard to leave. Our Flying Doctors team regrouped, the mass of us heading for the ambulances in the bay and then back to Wilson. We needed to restock the ambulances and the equipment bags and prepare for the next trip. Michael put the defective pediatric bag valve mask in a plastic bag to begin a patient safety investigation. With luck, we would learn something important from this error.

A few days after that call, I was reading in the bright sun outside the hangar at Wilson when Jana, one of the nurses who had worked in dispatch on that fateful night, walked by my chair and stopped. She had just returned to Flying Doctors' headquarters from Kenyatta Hospital and wondered if I had heard the good news about the little boy. All was well, she said. In the children's ward, she had seen the boy walking the halls, slowly, holding his mother's hand. His abdomen was bandaged and covered in tape, but he was alive and already up and moving around.

The surgeons had taken him to the OR soon after we arrived and had fixed his torn liver, sutured a torn section of intestine, and undertaken a splenectomy to remove his pulverized spleen. They had continued the regimen of antibiotics we had administered, as he had developed a nasty infection in his belly. A day after he arrived at the hospital, he was taken off the ventilator. The floor nurses were optimistic that he would be discharged home after a few more days of observation.

I smiled and thought about how our lives had collided and how he was just getting started in life. It occurred to me that he would never know how close he had come to dying. Years from now, maybe when he is sitting at home with his family, someone will point to his scars and ask how he got them. He won't remember; he will have been too young when it all happened. Any recollections he might have when he's older will probably be of his parents or sisters. He'll have no idea the two of us ever met. We'll certainly never meet again.

As a frequent witness to the epilogue to these sorts of disasters, I can tell you that one's life can change in an instant. It's not a platitude. It's the way these sorts of things work. Your life can be irrevocably altered by the smallest mishap, the smallest miscalculation in timing. One event unleashes a sequence of subsequent decisions and responses, and everything hinges on getting those decisions and responses right.

We are fragile beings. Most of us need to maintain

an illusion of control, an affirmation that we are masters of our own destiny. Only rarely, when terrible things happen, and if we are honest with ourselves, will we admit that some heartbreakingly important moments fall one way or an awful other based on nothing more than the smallest whims. Just capricious fortune. The universe will remind us that it's all so tenuous.

SOMEWHERE IMPORTANT

Although I had no idea what would come of it, the journey seemed portentous, the fulfillment of some vague yearning that occupied liminal recesses of my mind.

— Dr. Tom Rees, co-founder, AMREF

In 1956, three reconstructive surgeons gathered over drinks on the slopes of Mount Kilimanjaro to discuss establishing a medical charity that would care for East Africans. Sir Archibald "Archie" McIndoe, Sir Michael Wood, and Dr. Tom Rees were friends who shared a love for and a commitment to Africa. They would collaborate to form the Flying Doctors of East Africa.

Sir Archibald was one of the world's leading reconstructive surgeons during World War II. As Chief Surgeon for the British Royal Air Force, he had performed thousands of operations on young British pilots who were burned during combat. After the war, Sir Archibald bought a farm in Tanzania. He invited two former trainees—Dr. Michael Wood, an Englishman, and American Dr. Tom Rees—to join him in providing surgery to a needy population.

In the 1950s, few people living in remote areas of Africa had access to medical treatment. The three surgeons came up with a plan to bring health care to the remote hospitals by flying doctors in small single-engine planes into the bush. They also developed a shortwave radio network to link these facilities to Nairobi, which served as a hub.

Sir Archibald died of a sudden heart attack in 1960. Dr. Wood continued his work in Africa, as a surgeon and executive, until the early 1980s; he died in 1987. The last founder, Dr. Tom Rees, spent forty years splitting time between New York and Africa, where he continued to fly annual missions to hospitals deep in Tanzania and Kenya to perform surgery. He would repair cleft palates, graft burns, repair vaginal fistulas, and treat hyena wounds,

wounds from arrows, and rhino goring injuries.

The founders grew Flying Doctors into what became known as AMREF, the African Medical Research and Education Foundation. That organization became the Flying Doctors' parent organization, and it would eventually become one of the largest Non-Governmental Organizations in Africa.

In the early days, the doctors flew themselves in small Cessnas and Pipers to dirt landing strips across Africa. Children would greet the plane with excitement, and the doctors would be welcomed into the village. There, they would operate in bush hospitals, using ether for anesthesia—or, in some cases, slugs of scotch. One famous flying doctor, Dr. Anne Spoerry, was an internist who was estimated to have seen over half a million patients in the forty-nine years she flew across Kenya in her self-piloted Cessna. A big-hearted curmudgeon, she traveled alone, with only a medical bag and a pistol (in case things got funny).

Over the years, AMREF continued its program of sending specialists to rural hospitals. They began to develop skill in community health and disease control programs while also aggressively developing capacity as an air ambulance/air evacuation service. Flying Doctors became renowned globally as the only organization that could reliably get in and out of rural Africa. They had intimate knowledge of the hospitals and the runways, and the dirt strips and fields that could be used for landings. They also had an ear to the ground and were often the first to hear of political troubles, brewing coups, and regional instabilities that could prevent a rescue flight.

Flying Doctors became the best option, if not the only option, for medical evacuations out of the remotest areas of Africa, and they began to offer repatriation flights from Africa to Europe and North America—trips in which foreign visitors to Africa would be returned to their home countries. Most of these flights were billed to insurance. Some were cash pay, though, and others were provided free through the group's charity fund.

Unlike the early years of tiny Cessnas and Pipers, by 2008, when I first flew with Flying Doctors, medical calls were handled using one of three types of plane that were chosen according to the needs of time, distance, and runway length: single-engine Cessna Caravans were used for rescues utilizing small dirt strips in the bush; twin- engine Beechcraft King Air planes were used for rescues covering shorter distances and for larger dirt strips; and a Citation jet was used for evacuations from larger cities and distant locations. Two pilots, a nurse, and usually a doctor would be scrambled for each rescue. Most of the doctors were Kenyans, but there was sometimes a visiting physician staffing the roster, usually a European specialist in anesthesia or intensive care medicine—and, occasionally, a Canadian or American emergency medicine specialist. We were there to exchange medical best practices from around the world. Flying Doctors won several international awards and a well-deserved reputation for excellence. The quality of care was uniformly excellent.

At the end of 2008, I met Tom Rees for a drink in Santa Fe, New Mexico, not long after I returned to the United States from my first trip as a flying doctor. Tom had invited me to join him after I had sent him an unsolicited email. In it, I'd written that I was a young emergency medicine doctor, recently out of training and just back from my first trip with AMREF. I also said that I would love to speak with him if he might be open to it.

Tom had been a glamorous and accomplished American plastic surgeon with a thriving practice in aesthetic surgery in New York. He was notoriously charismatic, with movie-star looks. He was rumored to have done all the facelifts and nose jobs for the most important American socialites. He'd also published hundreds of articles and book chapters, and been the president of his national surgical organization.

Tom and his wife, the model Nan Rees, had retired to New Mexico years earlier. Tom suggested that we meet at the bar of an elegant restaurant located on fashionable Canyon Road, not too far from the safety-net teaching hospital where I was working. At the bar, we ordered glasses of wine. Tom's stories of caring for patients in Africa were all perseverance and grit. He was informal, wise, and deeply experienced. I remember feeling that I was in the presence of greatness; he seemed to be an example of how a purposeful medical life could be lived.

I asked Tom why he had spent forty years in Africa. He began by describing his work in Kenya as "seeking his bliss," something he also had written in his memoir. I should have stopped and asked him right then what he meant—it would have saved me a lot of time. But I didn't, and Tom paused for a few moments and looked at me with his piercing eyes. He asked me why *I* had chosen to be a flying doctor. It was a fair question. Medevac work was dirty, dangerous, and unglamorous. One needed a reason to show up.

I didn't communicate this well at the time, but—

much like Tom—my decision to become a flying doctor was unconscious on some level, a vague yearning. I explained that I was at a professional impasse and was seeking something more from medicine.

I was hesitant to complain to this giant of a man, this exemplar of accomplishment and stoicism. So, I explained how I had read his autobiography before leaving for Africa and how it had captured my imagination. How I was just out of training when I finally admitted to myself that emergency medicine—my chosen vocation, the goal that had propelled me for a decade—ultimately hadn't turned out to be what I had hoped for.

I'd become an attending doctor at a time when the American health care system was at peak crisis, taking a toll on both patients and caregivers. Costs were unaffordable. This was before Obamacare passed; many, many patients had no insurance and few places to go for care. Some patients had complex needs—psychiatric concerns, substance abuse, complex illnesses—that weren't being managed in long-term settings. The emergency department had become the fallback, a place of both first and last resort, a diner with an unlimited menu serving all things to all customers. We were open to all, and our waiting room never emptied.

It wasn't the diversity of problems that was the issue; the ability to meet those needs was the department's main attraction. Rather, it was the constant triage, the endless shortcuts and corner-cutting that allowed us to get to the next patient and then the next. These shortcuts weren't just a short-term adaptation to a disaster; they had become routine, lest we didn't move fast enough to identify the next catastrophe walking through our doors. I was left feeling like I never provided care that met my own internal standards.

I also realized that the emergency medicine staff were on our own. The hospital system oligopolies and their self-interested leaders had other priorities. They wanted to attract well-insured patients with lucrative problems by building opulent cancer and cardiac "centers of excellence," but there had been no such investment in the emergency department. Elsewhere, private equity had begun to buy physician groups, pushing "productivity" and patients per hour as their "key performance indicators."

I began to reflect on what was called "rack rage," my staring at the never-ending long line of clipboards on the counter, each representing a patient to be seen. The cockroach administrators knew that the doctors and nurses would see all the patients no matter how bad they made things, even when staffing wasn't adequate. Such was medical professionalism. They knew that the clinicians would never say no, would never skip work, would never pause for a break if there were patients to be seen. The system was shitty and extractive and profit-generating, and it totally depended on the good-will of doctors and nurses who held everything together for the least-fortunate patients, using twine and tape if necessary. The doctors and nurses got screwed, and the patients got screwed worse. Above us, the executives at the insurance companies and the big health care systems haggled and bartered and justified their large salaries by pointing at the complexity they had to manage—which was, of course, a Byzantine system of their own making.

These days, psychologists might claim that my colleagues and I had experienced moral injury, the diagnosis originally given to soldiers forced by their profession to act in ways that were contrary to their consciences. The term hadn't yet been applied to health care in 2008 (though it would be later), but it was apropos. I was acutely aware that medicine, for me, had strayed from the ideals I had subscribed to and believed in: the art of one-on-one healing, honesty, and ministry. Mostly, medicine lacked the intimacy I wanted to experience with patients in their time of need—an opportunity to spend time as a healer, a chance to get to know someone for a bit, to share in their journey. I chafed at what the business of medicine had done to us, and to our patients.

After all the years I had spent preparing for this moment, emergency medicine had turned out to be a serious disappointment. To put it honestly, I was defeated.

But, of course, I didn't say all that to Tom Rees. I was too stoic, too embarrassed to have found myself in such a powerless position, and too proud. I finally said to him that traveling to Africa to become a flying doctor was an opportunity to practice a different type of medicine, one that felt important and real, and which let me feel a kind of professional intimacy with strangers, under the most challenging circumstances. I paused, giving it more thought. Then, I told Tom that I had wanted to experience powerful beauty and gratitude; I wanted to feel like I could chart a course autonomously, according to my own wits and decisions, far from the thumbs of powerful people with misaligned incentives. Each patient was a lesson. I think he understood.

An unexpected personal reckoning and some good fortune had put me in the back of that African air ambulance in Tanzania, working to save the life of a little boy. It's a good place to begin this story, but it wasn't the beginning of my journey. That much longer path started nearly two decades earlier, in a rural village in upstate New York. I followed that path across America and then to South America, the Middle East, and—finally— Africa. It brought me, then, to the back of a medevac plane, where there was much I needed to figure out.

LEARNING TO FLY

It might be said that a great unstated reason for travel is to find places that exemplify where one has been happiest. Looking for idealized versions of home—indeed, looking for the perfect memory.

— Paul Theroux

A Canadian friend who had spent twenty years working abroad once told me that there were three types of people who left to work far from home: there were those who were running from something; those who were looking for an adventure; and those who were in it for the money. In my case, it certainly wasn't about the money—at Flying Doctors, there was none. But my reasons for joining the group in 2008 hadn't been totally altruistic. My motivations lay somewhere between adventure and escapism, and probably closer to the latter. I needed room to think. To me, the most obvious place to make sense of things, to take stock, was on the road. I yearned to travel.

I'm a wanderer. I've always been one. I am peripatetic, more comfortable when moving, inclined to seek unfamiliar places when I need to look inside myself. I'd long identified with my favorite author, travel writer Paul Theroux, and did so even after reading the unflattering exposé his former wife had written about their marriage. "Many travelers are boys who never grow up," she wrote in her book, "in whom all those characteristics that are normal in a youth of seventeen or eighteen are continued into later life." I transcribed and starred the passage in my journal for future follow-up, maybe on a foreign trip.

Ending up at Flying Doctors was a beautiful result of sheer luck, a serendipitous cold call. A distant family friend, who was a pilot, had worked with an African medical non-governmental organization in the 1990s. I vaguely remembered that he had moved to Africa and had written a book about his experiences, so I looked him up online. He had worked for an organization called

Flying Doctors. When I looked further into the NGO, I saw that they had a visiting physician program. Without much deliberation, I sent an unsolicited email and my résumé to Flying Doctors in Nairobi.

I'm no believer in the paranormal, but I've always found that when things are meant to be, when they are supposed to happen, the pieces somehow seem to come together faster and more easily than expected. Life had been like that for me: when opportunities were not right, getting in had been like pulling teeth. Inevitably, when later viewed from a wiser, more dispassionate perspective, I could see that they'd been all wrong for me. But the right opportunities, the ones my mother would, with a wink, call "bashert"—a Yiddish word meaning "preordained" or "destined to be"—were frictionless. My mother knew me better than anyone; maybe they were less of a surprise to her than to me. But somehow these ideal opportunities always simply slid into place.

So it went with Flying Doctors. I received an email response to my query the next day from Dr. Beata, the hyper-competent German intensivist who oversaw the service. Flying Doctors had an immediate need for a visiting physician; she wondered if I would come to Nairobi for a one-month rotation, starting in a month. I took thirty seconds to commit. There was no question that I would go. I knew there was nothing that I'd rather do, no other place else that I *should* be. I booked a flight and applied for my Kenyan medical license that same day.

The etymology of "bashert" is the German word, "beschert," which means bestowed or gifted, often referring to the act of receiving divine gifts. Flying Doctors was, in retrospect, one of those transcendent gifts. I'd had many more enormously lucky breaks along the way—times when, against the odds, an unexpected door would open and I would humbly walk through. Flying Doctors was the capstone to a series of earlier, longer-term opportunities where I learned how to doctor a diverse population of patients outside the hospital, on the streets.

Somewhere around 1991, I treated my first patient. I was an emergency medical technician (EMT) and a college student in rural New York state. I had joined the small town's volunteer ambulance service in my first year on campus. It was a pure fluke, an opportunity I had seen in a booklet of volunteer activities the university had mailed to freshmen in the weeks before classes began. In that first year, I went to university during the day and took community college classes at night to become an

EMT. Later, in my junior year, I took more advanced community college classes to become an advanced-level EMT. While the university would ultimately award me a bachelor's degree, in philosophy and religion, I really spent my four years off-campus at the ambulance barn, training with medical equipment and responding to emergency calls. At twenty, before I could legally drink beer, I had achieved a position of real responsibility. Eventually, I became the Crew Chief, the most senior medic on a call, and I could administer complex medications, place airway devices, and perform emergency procedures for the patients we served.

Even as a college student, I recognized that there was something human and profound about meeting people in their homes, engaging with their problems, and bearing their loads, at least for a short time. Ambulance calls offered unique access to other people; they were an invitation into the lives of random strangers who were usually far different from the college students I met in the cloistered environments I knew. Going out on a call demanded that I engage on a patient's terms, not mine.

Once, on a morning call, I had one of those moments upon which one's whole life narrative pivots. I had been on-call during the hot summer days when the students were gone, and the townspeople were mostly on vacation. At 4 a.m., my pager alerted me to a cardiac arrest in a small village we covered, south of town. Like usual, I jumped into a uniform shirt and ran to my car and quickly drove the half a mile to the ambulance barn. An EMT, a driver, and I got into the boxy diesel ambulance and drove down the two-lane highway. As we sped past well-maintained driveways and lawns, the ambulance's red lights reflected off the windows of the houses that lined the road.

The village's tiny fire department had arrived before us. I could see their pickup in the driveway of a double-wide trailer set a few hundred feet off the road. We pulled in and walked up the steps into the simple home. My eyes took in the dried flowers in vases and the brown wall-to-wall carpet, overstuffed lounge recliners, old pictures of young men in uniform, and new pictures of children in pink Barbie shirts and Mickey Mouse ears. The home's occupant, a woman in her late seventies, had filled the shelves of her curio cabinet with Beanie Baby collectibles and ribbons from the county fair. I felt I knew her just from looking around. But now this woman was on the floor, lying between the couch and the coffee table, face-up, receiving CPR from her next-door neighbors who were members of the village's volunteer fire department. She was a fleshy woman, and her hair was permed. Her cheeks were sunken, and because her dentures were still in a cup in the bathroom, the firemen's ventilations sounded as effective as blowing raspberries on a baby's belly. I inserted an oral airway and then checked her carotid artery for a pulse. I felt nothing.

I was the only medic, the only one able to deliver the advanced care needed. I moved as if on autopilot. First, I unbuttoned the woman's floral-print housedress and attached the cardiac monitor to her chest wall. I could see the chaotic non-pattern of a heart spasming wildly. I took the paddles off our suitcase-sized Lifepak 5 defibrillator, built in 1976 when I was a toddler. I smeared them with conductive gel. Then, I leaned over the woman, yelled "Clear," and delivered shock after shock to her chest. Her body jerked off the floor with every shock, until finally the green analog cardioscope showed short but regular beats. The woman now had a pulse, and her skin began to warm slightly. She began to breathe on her own. It was a resurrection.

The firemen carried the woman out of the trailer on a stretcher and brought our equipment down the front steps to the ambulance. Inside the rig, after five tries,

I was finally able to get an IV flowing. Her arms were marked and bloody from my efforts. I then administered the medications listed in the protocol book. Flying down the two-lane highway, we delivered the woman, quite alive, to the rural community hospital ER.

Her son, who lived just down the road from her and was the father of the little girl with the Barbie shirt, arrived at the ER shortly after we did. He was a tall man, wearing work boots and a blue shirt with his name stitched in script on its breast. He stopped me in the hallway, clasped my hands in his, and thanked me.

Still flooded with adrenalin from the call, I ran through the events in my head over and over, hoping I had done the right things. I was a barely-competent college student wearing a polyester shirt with patches on it and a leather holster with a pair of trauma shears attached to my belt. My legs were shaking to the point that I could hardly stand. I clutched the back of a wheelchair for support.

When we had restocked the rig and finished the paperwork, I sat quietly in the small hospital cafeteria, in the back of the single-story hospital. It was too late in the morning—and I was too wired—to consider going home to bed. So, I drank bad coffee from a vending machine. I was only twenty, but I had saved a life. It was a divine gift.

That was when I knew I would become a doctor.

The decision to do so seems obvious to me now, but at the time, it was not. It was not something I had ever considered.

I got through college without any reflection on or consideration of what I would do next. I had been a lazy student with a C-average transcript, someone with a smoking habit and vague thoughts of becoming a writer. But I realized in that cafeteria that I had found what felt like my purpose. I had stumbled onto it quite accidentally and outside of the formal curriculum. At the same time, I worried that maybe it was too late. I had taken no science classes beyond the single course requirement for which I'd spent a semester looking at rocks in a lab. My grades wouldn't get me into a cosmetology program.

But by some miracle—one of many in my extraordinarily fortunate life—I was accepted into a post-college science program. I knew there was no margin for error, and I became an A student overnight. While I waited to apply to medical school, I completed a master's degree in public health, concentrating in international health.

And then, one afternoon, a thin letter arrived in the

mail. I would enter medical school that fall, at Jefferson in Philadelphia, four years later than most of my classmates. Getting accepted to med school was easily the biggest professional break of my life, a true act of grace.

A second break was landing in a residency slot, four years later, at a top program in emergency medicine. It was a program I had targeted with a laser focus. The University of Pittsburgh was a holy pilgrimage for anyone interested in prehospital medicine, which continued to be my area of interest. For three years, I was surrounded by an extraordinary group of doctors, truly the field's legends. They had invented CPR. They were the architects of the modern EMS system. And they took me in their hands and molded me in their image.

I had finally arrived.

Medicine usually happens in offices and hospitals that are unmistakably doctors' lairs; they are specifically designed to protect doctors' time and attention. But emergency care has nothing to do with doctors' conveniences. The delivery of emergency care is set according to each patient's needs. It is an intimate and intense specialty, requiring an enormous degree of sensitivity. To be good at it, to be really tuned in to the patient and his problem and to not make mistakes, requires a certain humility, a willingness to meet patients on their own terms, and even a vulnerability on the part of the doctor. This is true everywhere in emergency medicine. It is even more true in international emergency medicine, where language and status, skin color, and power can create huge barriers. Diagnosing a patient overseas is like losing a sense. There, a doctor's ability to communicate and treat is profoundly restricted—by language, fear, a patient's deference, and their profound gratitude.

When I graduated residency, I chose to stay on for an additional year to complete a fellowship in international emergency medicine. I spent the next year living out of a suitcase, studying tropical medicine and infectious disease in Peru, working in the Caribbean, and then finally working in the Middle East. This fellowship led to a full-time job as the first medical director for the Qatari national ambulance service, based in Doha.

Qatar, in those days, was in an anabolic, post-pubescent phase. Fueled by hydrocarbon money, the race was on to build not only bragging rights, but also core infrastructure: hospitals, schools, restaurants and shopping centers, sports stadiums, and airports were all under construction while I was there in 2006. It was a country making up for lost time, and it was replacing old buildings and dusty lots with huge skyscrapers and plush resorts with astonishing rapidity. Doha reminded me of the Vegas strip—miles of nothing, then suddenly bright lights and fancy cars being driven badly.

The Qataris paid me well to develop a clinically strong ambulance service. So, I did. A wide-eyed, can-do doctor, I became the service's first official medical director. It was, I think, a role that no Qatari doctor would take on; it was an unglamorous, gritty job, even blue-collar, and probably beneath their dignity. I wrote care protocols inspired by high-performing US systems, and I responded to road crashes and fainting cases and broken arms with multinational crews—some EMTs from the Philippines and Tunisia, others from Morocco and Syria, and a collection of odd but fun characters from Australia, the UK, and the US.

In Doha, I was a long-term guest at a high-rise hotel that had good views of the Persian Gulf. There were plenty of faux-gold gilded couches, and endless chandeliers, but it was a comfortable place with decent air conditioning. There was a nice pool, and a fellow distributing premium dates from a wooden box in the lobby. As I had no real plans, no illusions that I would be in Qatar for long, it suited me fine. I was, for all intents, an itinerant, living in a hotel designed for short-term stays. I did make some changes: I replaced the single-use shampoo bottles provided by the hotel with large ones from the grocery store, filled the minibar with large cases of soda, and added a desktop computer and router. This setup, with its impermanence, was exactly as I wanted it. It required no commitment on my part.

After a couple of years, I got to know the routine and became part of the fabric of the city. Mornings, just before sunrise and before the mourning doves began to mourn, I laid in my hotel bed and tuned my two-way radio to the ambulance dispatch channel. Often—so often as to be a regular occurrence—I was able to catch an ambulance being sent to the Industrial Area. As its name implied, the area did contain a number of warehouses and factories. But that was only half the story. Most of the Industrial Area was taken up by a series of sprawling labor camps. These camps were home to tens of thousands of laborers from Bangladesh, Nepal, the Philippines, and other desperately poor places.

It always seemed to me that this collection of warehouses and cement factories and massive labor camps should have been called, "the accommodation area with some industry." Calling it the Industrial Area was to use a euphemism which obscured the reality that the area was the most densely packed and most biologically active square of land in Qatar.

Workers lived and ate and slept in those camps, often ten to a room. And there were often two different groups of men—the night shift and those who worked days— who shared the sweltering accommodations. These anonymous sweating men, all dressed alike in blue jumpsuits, were there to work. Given language barriers and their desire not to stand out, they said nothing except to their own countrymen. They did what they were told and put up with staggering heat for a meager paycheck, which they dutifully transferred home from exchange shops when they were let out for a few hours on Fridays.

I lived in Doha, in that hotel, for two years and could predict, almost to the minute, when the Industrial Area emergency calls would start to come in. My clock was synchronized with theirs; wakeup was always at five in the morning, because the shifts swapped at six. The foremen always called for an ambulance a few minutes after the breakfast bell was rung and after the workers had crawled from bed into their jumpsuits and assembled to go to work. The timing meant that I needed to be out of the shower by five thirty—because that left enough time for the workers to find their roommates dead in bed and call the medics, and for the medics to call me.

Bangungut is a Tagalog word combining the words "rising" and "groaning." Arabs know it as *khapoos*. The colloquialism refers to "nightmare" deaths in which a young man, typically Asian, will groan in his sleep and then suddenly, and usually unremarkably and without anyone noticing, die. These deaths were caused by a genetic susceptibility which caused sudden cardiac death in young Asian men. It has been formally described in recent years as Sudden Unexplained Nocturnal Death Syndrome but is probably still formally unexplained. One theory, though, holds that it hinges on faulty sodium channels in the cells of the heart. Over the years, scientists in Asia recognized that *Bangungut* deaths happened to farmers and heavy laborers; and those scientists have come to believe that heat, dehydration, and intense exertion magnify the genetic problems.

When the emergency calls came in from the Industrial Area, the ambulance service's crews would respond. They would reach the bedside and apply the cardiac monitor to the patient. They would then observe a perfectly flat cardiac tracing. Next, they would look for rigor mortis.

The medics would then call me on the radio, almost always between five thirty and six, and ask for permission to declare death. None of these people were ever resuscitated. In most cases, they'd been dead for hours.

Dying in the Industrial Area was an empty end. The typical worker's death went unnoticed, even by the roommates who lay in exhausted sleep in their stacked rows. What happened next depended on whether their employer followed the rules; if he did, after receiving the paperwork from the pathologist, the worker's body would be sent home in the cargo hold of a Qatar Airways flight, along with any back wages and maybe a small gratuity. Other times, an embassy in Doha would be called upon to intervene to get even this modest accommodation from the shameless employers. Some embassies were more effective in their arm-twisting than others. The Filipinos ran their embassy like a Teamsters local. If an employer behaved badly, their supply of Filipino workers would be cut off.

It was easy to hit out at the Qatari authorities for lax safety standards and poor workers' rights—and much of the criticism was deserved. But it's also true that Qatar was on overdrive, making up for lost time, and it barely had a regulatory handle on the thriving market for cheap labor, a major export that supported millions of people in the developing world. So, like most things, it was complicated.

I came to understand that it was easy to spend time outraged, especially when considering geopolitics, or politics in general. But outrage is often an excuse to take no action or an opportunity to position oneself to push boulders up hills—which must be done selectively. There is ambiguity in the world. Qatar taught me that to be a fully formed adult, one needed to properly digest an issue before taking a stand; and even then, it was smart to recognize that an opinion may not reflect the full dimension of an issue. If one didn't put in this work, it was possible to become easy prey for propogandists, social media "haters," and human resource executives.

As a doctor, I didn't need to straddle the space between analytic paralysis and gullibility; I could just show up at work and do what I could to respond to calls with energy; to see patients enthusiastically; and to try, incrementally, to improve health care on a systems level. In my corner of the Middle East, I vowed that EMS care would be excellent and we would treat all patients to the limits of our skills, and we would nudge the broken parts of the system gently but consistently to effect change.

Show up, don't be shrill, listen, and understand.

I checked out of the hotel for good in 2008. After two years, my wanderlust had turned to loneliness. I knew that the gig in the Middle East wasn't a career, but more an engaging detour from full-time clinical practice. I also knew that I didn't want to do full-time emergency medicine. After a few months, I sent my resignation and returned to the US with a stack of suitcases, some engraved plaques, and a personalized glass oryx desk pen set in a cardboard box.

Yet, I did not leave Qatar *for something.* And when I arrived back in the US, I found myself wondering, "What next?" The chance to work with Flying Doctors was a liminal opportunity. I was free of the attachments I would later create for myself as a professor, startup leader, executive, and eventual spouse and father with a lawn. Being of service in Kenya seemed like it would help me figure out what was next. It was the right path forward.

There is a clichéd history of Westerners heading to Africa to get lost. But the reality is that no Westerner has any idea how the place works. It's not home. You don't speak the language. You have no real part in the daily machinery. You're tangential and most certainly a casual observer of lives you don't meaningfully understand—which doesn't invalidate travelling or trying to be of service. But you need to understand that foreign places are foreign, and you shouldn't romanticize them too much. Lives are hard everywhere, and maybe more so in Africa.

The reasons for my trip were quite pragmatic. In my case, Kenya was less about escapism and more about a desire to focus. I wanted to ground myself in the essentials of medicine. I wanted to dispense with the superfluousness of administrators, their monetization of everything decent, and the unreasonable demands of the modern ER. I wanted to work, intimately, with patients.

Africa was an opportunity to test my clinical abilities, alone, in the most challenging circumstances, and reaffirm my self-sufficiency. I found all of this and more—indescribably more—at Flying Doctors.

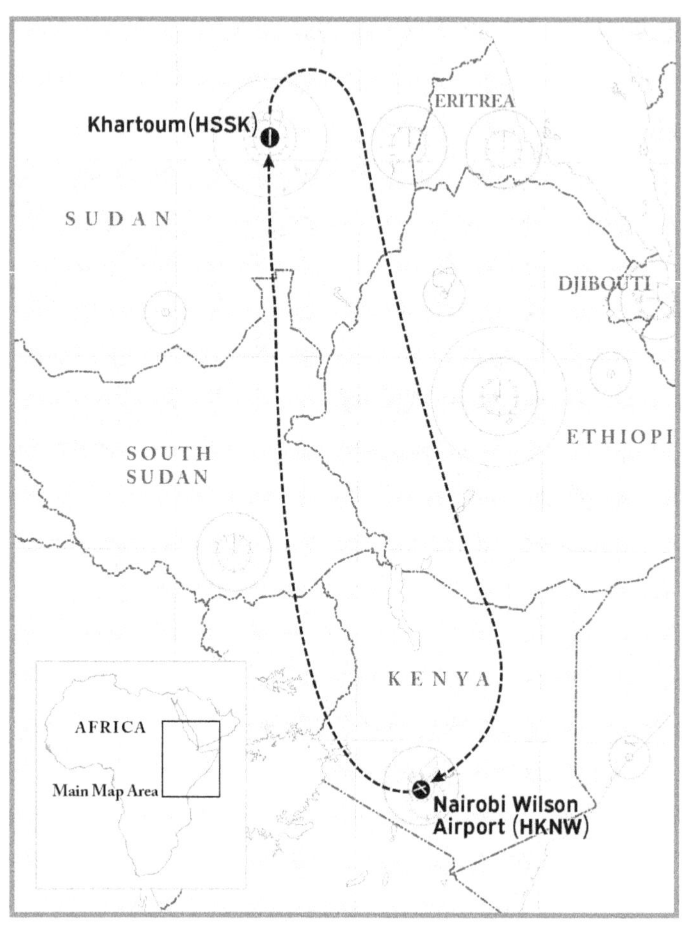

Evacuation from Khartoum, Sudan, using a Citation

STRONGMAN

"We're governed by our religion. And our own religion prevents us completely from assault, from violating properties, even general, public properties, or even affecting the environment, like the cutting of a tree.

— Omar al Bashir,
President of Sudan from 1989–2019

A battered pickup truck intercepted us on the taxiway in Khartoum, Sudan. The driver drove too quickly toward our wing and then turned on his yellow flashing lights and pulled in front of our slowly taxiing jet. He impatiently led us to the edge of the tarmac. He was unnecessary, and it was a show; the pilots were there regularly and knew exactly where we had to go. But the men in the truck had been told to keep a close eye on us, and so they did, with equal measures of carelessness and aggressiveness. We pulled into the parking area, next to the international terminal. The truck did a quick U- turn and parked, facing us. Inside, the men—police, I imagined—stared at us and then opened their windows and, only meters from the fuel trucks, lit cigarettes and started gossiping.

The pilots shut down the engines and opened the plane door. Sudan was stunningly hot and dry, a dramatic change from the plane's air conditioning and that morning's humid conditions in Kenya. Outside the plane, our "fixer" was sweating and impatient; he had been waiting for us in a basic Toyota sedan.

The fixer was a brash and inelegant man—bearded, short, and short tempered. He was holding a clipboard; he did the paperwork and managed the fees. It was he who would lubricate the officials by feeding them the money they needed to keep the whole operation moving. He was our regular guy in Sudan, and his not-so-secret weapon was cash, which he used to keep the planes flying and people and papers in motion. Men like our fixer sit at the intersections of cultures, selling their knowledge and connections. He made no show of pretending to be a friend. His loyalties were clear. His work for us was purely transactional, and we all knew it.

Ongoing Western sanctions against the Sudanese government had made foreign banks and credit cards anachronisms; no external money was supposed to flow into the country. The Sudanese were being punished by the Americans for being state sponsors of terrorism, apparently for harboring terrorists. Sudan had adapted by becoming a cash-only economy, so we paid for our fuel in cash, paid our fixer in cash, and then handed him money to handle every other random fee in cash. The captain carried it in a bag. The rules were clear: we could only use US hundred-dollar bills, nothing older than a 2003 series, and nothing wrinkled or torn.

As emergency evacuations went, this one was straightforward. The UN had called the Flying Doctors' call center and base at Wilson airport in Nairobi and asked for an emergency air ambulance transfer from Khartoum. Nurse John and I had packed the plane full of medical equipment: canvas equipment bags, ventilators, blood coolers, splints and IV pumps, and bags of various medications. After the pilots checked the weather and filed a flight plan in Nairobi, we taxied to the runway and then headed north on the Citation jet.

John and I were now old hands at preparing the equipment. Before we even arrived at the airport, our operations team and security teams had made all the necessary plans. Every detail had been considered, down to the bag of sandwiches and thermos of coffee they had sent in an insulated bag.

Standing outside on the concrete tarmac in Khartoum, we stared across the shimmering air at the distant gate. We were impatient and coming apart from the heat. In the distance, we could see the UN ambulance carrying our patient as it passed through the airport gates. It came closer and then stopped near our right wing. A distinguished, balding, thin man, maybe fifty years old, extracted himself from the back of the van and joined us on the tarmac, watched carefully by the secret policemen. He was the local UN doctor, a long-timer who was wearing Chinese running shoes and a stained white coat. He had his UN identification hanging from a shoelace looped around his neck.

Dr. Painda was Afghani and experienced in matters of war. His home country had been in a state of civil war since the 1970s. To make ends meet, he had left his family— first to work for the UN in Darfur, a desolate war-torn region in South Sudan, and then later to work near Khartoum, which was by all measures a better posting. His life seemed lonely and dangerous, and I suspected that he was miserably paid for his efforts. Once a year, Painda got back to Afghanistan after paying an exorbitant fee to the fly-by-night airlines which ran the Sudan-Dubai-Kabul route.

As I dug into the transfer notes he had brought, Painda made an offhand comment that militiamen had shot out the windows of the guesthouse where he was staying a few weeks earlier. He had calmly reassured his fellow guests that it was random fire from undisciplined teens and pointed out where to sit to avoid the worst of it. His comment was apropos of nothing and very casual. I guessed he would know.

In Khartoum, we all huddled on the tarmac because none of us could safely or legally leave the airport. None of us had visas. And Sudan was, by any measure, no place for an American. There had been assassination attempts against US diplomats in Khartoum; America was far from popular. Our solution was to rely on the patients to come to us, which they did in the relatively protected confines of the transit area of the international airport. It was a deal probably pulled together by our cranky candyman.

Candymen were how things got done—not just for us, but for everyone in Sudan. I never asked how much of the cash the captain dispensed was for official fees and fuel and how much was used to grease wheels. But I guessed that payments beyond those officially required were routine. Sudan was notoriously corrupt—it was among the most corrupt nations in the world. The World Bank also rated Sudan among the worst-governed states, using several measures: political stability, rule of law, regulatory environment, government effectiveness, and control of corruption. Transparency International, an NGO, prepared an annual Corruption Perceptions Index which reported the perceived levels of public-sector corruption in 180 countries. Scores ranged from zero (most corrupt) to ten (least corrupt). In 2008, Sudan had a 1.6/10 rating. Of the 180 surveyed countries, only Afghanistan, Haiti, Myanmar, Iraq, and Somalia rated lower. Sudan's scores had been worsening for several years.

Most average Sudanese people felt this pinch. In Sudan, petty corruption was pervasive. This meant that citizens in one of the least developed countries in the world were expected to pay bribes to the police, the customs bureau, tax authorities, and land services. It meant that government appointments were made based on political connections, and that court decisions were subject to political manipulations.

Much of this dysfunction seemed to be top-down. For years, Sudan had been run by a strongman, Omar al-Bashir. He had taken power in 1993 in the latest in a series of military coups that had installed and deposed leaders since 1969, when Sudan first claimed independence. Al-Bashir led the long fight for independence in South Sudan, which resulted in the displacement and deaths of millions of southerners. He was being pursued by the International Criminal Court for claims of genocide. They alleged that he had also siphoned billions of dollars out of the country for personal use. For their part, the Americans considered Sudan a state sponsor of terrorism that harbored Islamic terrorists. They had imposed sanctions and banned US companies from doing business in the country; there had been no US Ambassador in Sudan since 1996.

On the tarmac, we got ready to load and go. Our patient, lying in the back of the UN ambulance, was a late-middle-aged and slightly dusty Ghanian UN worker who was doing relief work in Sudan. He was bleeding—there was a hole somewhere in his stomach. I was not sure if treatment wasn't available in Khartoum, or whether it simply wasn't trusted to be good enough. Regardless, he wanted to be transferred to the relative safety of Nairobi, which was why we were there.

The ground staff helped lift our patient and the stretcher onto the rack installed in the plane. I could hear the stretcher click into place. Once it was secured, the patient looked up and shook Dr. Painda's hand quite sincerely and gratefully.

Gastric bleeds are diagnosed and treated by passing a camera down the patient's throat. The doctor can determine the site of bleeding and use the scope to plug the hole. In a really bad case—say, where a large vein or artery has ruptured—the bleeding can be profuse enough that a patient repeatedly fills their stomach with blood. When the stomach hits capacity, it contracts, and the patient projectile-vomits candy-apple red blood. Our patient's bleed was less urgent, though, a slow ooze.

We had no endoscope, and all we could do on the ride to Nairobi was to continue to drain his stomach. One end of the tube sat in his belly; the other end hung on his face and was attached to a length of suction line and a pump. The blood brought up through the tube was partly digested and had turned black and granulated. If things got much worse, we could give him a transfusion. To do that, we'd spike the cool, dark bag of O- negative blood that we carried in a festive, hard picnic cooler. The blood had to be kept cool; as such, it was surrounded by ice packs. We'd drip the new blood into a vein via one tube and suck it out from his stomach via another.

I don't remember what the patient and I talked about as we loaded—maybe nothing given the uncomfortable tube in his throat. But I remember he was pale despite the heat, and he had a fast pulse, though he was stable enough for the moment.

I climbed aboard the jet and shoved the small plastic bag with the patient's clothing and paperwork in it under the stretcher mattress, and then we watched through the window as Dr. Painda climbed into the dusty ambulance and was driven back to the airport gates, back to his life in Sudan. Outside, near the tire blocks, the fixer dripped sweat and yelled and swore at the ground staff and swung his clipboard in arcs and gesticulated at the pilot. Happy to be rid of him, we closed and locked the door. The pilots started the engines, and we received clearance to taxi. It was an in-and-out.

The evacuation flight to Nairobi allowed for an hour

or two of contemplation. Our patient fell asleep quickly. We had positioned the stretcher so he was reclined at an angle. He was covered by a white sheet. Attached nearby, a suction cannister periodically filled with small spurts of dark blood from his tube, but not much else was going on. The lights in the jet were dim, and John, ever energetic and competent, kept watch as we sipped Nescafé and I jotted down notes in the chart. Every so often, I would look at the monitor down by our patient's feet and see the reassuring EKG tracing and his vital signs, which cycled every few minutes.

In Sudan, thirty-two million people lived in a dysfunctional kleptocracy. Across the rest of North Africa—in Libya, Tunisia, Egypt, Syria—other people were in the same boat. I wasn't sure how the Sudanese, 97 percent who were observant Muslims, could rationalize this daily grind, given that corruption was explicitly prohibited in the Quran. I was sure that the contradiction weighed heavily; nobody wanted to live in a corrupt system, and doing so created a deep sense of instability. Yet, one way or the other, they went about their day figuring out how to survive or get a leg up. The corruption in Sudan flowed at all levels: from oil money being sent to a president's personal Swiss bank accounts to graft being passed to the lowest customs officials on the tarmac of the regional airport. It was insidious and toxic.

A simple explanation was that the only thing less desirable than living under a strongman president was a descent into chaos. Living in a failed state like Somalia would be worse, presumably, than suffering at the hands of an authoritarian kleptocrat. Power vacuums in Africa emerged when leadership changed, often violently and suddenly. Time and time again, across the continent, the perceived or actual vulnerability in a leader invited coups, which in no way guaranteed that the next government—if one emerged—would be better than the last. Often, they invited repressive military rule. And when strongman regimes fell, they fell quickly, because the country had limited internal governance capacity. Over the years, the leader would have deliberately weakened other political actors in order to reduce the chances of a challenge to his rule.

So that was the tradeoff. A strongman promised to maintain stability. He used state resources to buy loyalty, thereby enhancing his political power. Most of the Sudanese people learned to deal with the indignities of a corrupt system to avoid the greater evil of having no functioning government at all.

There had been 169 documented coup attempts in Africa since 1950, and more than 50 percent were successful. Sixty-eight percent of the autocrats who fell between 1946 and 2008 were victims of a coup d'état orchestrated from within government. Thirteen of the coups had happened in Sudan. To protect against such an event, Omar al-Bashir played different divisions of government against one another, creating internal rivalries. He enacted policies aimed at weakening civil society and threatening or undermining journalists, teachers, and other educated people.

How much longer would the Sudanese population tolerate such bad governance? Sudan's population was increasingly young, internet-connected, and idle. Sixty percent of the population was below the age of twenty-five, and the rate of unemployment was high among youth. In urban areas, 40 percent of youth had nothing to do. Many had given up looking for work. Paradoxically, Sudan's economy had grown significantly after the discovery of oil in 1999, but the country had missed the opportunity to diversify. Few of the funds made it to the people. Making matters even more difficult, the oil was found mostly in the disputed area of South Sudan, which was fighting for its independence, and which

Sudan would lose if South Sudan succeeded.

How much longer could the strongman keep the pot from boiling over?

Of course, I realized it was easy to hold opinions about democracy and freedom from afar while enjoying the relative immunity that a Western passport affords. A few years earlier, in Doha, I sat in a Turkish restaurant sharing kabobs and lavash with supervisors from the ambulance service. Yusef was a senior supervisor from Khartoum who had been in Doha for dozens of years. A bit older, educated and hardworking, he made enough to sponsor his wife and children on his visa. His kids were in an Arabic school; he didn't think he would ever go back.

Yusef and I had been discussing a recent medical rescue that the local news had covered in its typical style, which was a combination of bland and formal Indian prose and PR script. I mentioned to Yusef that I found the local *Gulf Times* shallow, lacking controversy and legitimate inquiry. They were never of critical of the authorities. It felt like a whitewash.

Yusef looked at me for a moment, carefully, gauging his words even though we'd known each other for a few years and he generally felt comfortable enough to speak directly and honestly. "The Doha papers," he told me, "are pillars of journalistic freedom in comparison to most places in the world. With respect," he said, "you have no idea what it is like to live in a true autocracy. In Sudan, you never discuss politics publicly. Conversations are a series of euphemisms. You have no idea who might report you to the police. No one has the freedom to hold or share an opinion about anything. You do what you can to keep your head low, and you figure out how to feed your family." To publicly oppose an autocracy demands an unimaginable amount of courage. That's how most of the world works.

I found myself somehow unequipped to deal with or fully internalize what he was saying. Yusef was right: I had no idea how it must feel to live in a place where the dreams I had for myself and for my family were totally at the mercy of forces of power I couldn't control. I had been raised to believe that I had the ability to change my circumstances, to advocate for myself, and to appeal to the rule of law. I believed in a system that would impartially hear my concerns and adjudicate them and safeguard my rights. Yusef's admonishment stung. He was right, of course. Nobody, given a choice, would pick kleptocracy or anarchy as forms of government. Good governance, democratic and otherwise, was a rare and valuable thing. His statements, and my reactions, were stark reminders of the importance of putting oneself—emotionally and practically—into the shoes of others before evaluating the circumstances in which people find themselves.

On our flight back to Nairobi, long lines of thunderstorms formed in the distance, well below the plane. Below us, South Sudan was dark and empty and at war. Unseen by us, perhaps, the killing nevertheless continued, just as it had done for years.

From the clouds, bolts of lightning emerged and jaggedly shot toward the ground every few seconds, a skittish and lethal show in yellow, brown, orange, and purple. At forty thousand feet, the curvature of the earth was very clear. The storm's power over the vast area made me feel small and insignificant.

The storm seemed a perfect and dangerous metaphor for the lands over which we passed. There were big forces at work across the region. Something was in the air; the countries of North Africa felt like a tinderbox. The people wanted better. What would change require? What would it take for better?

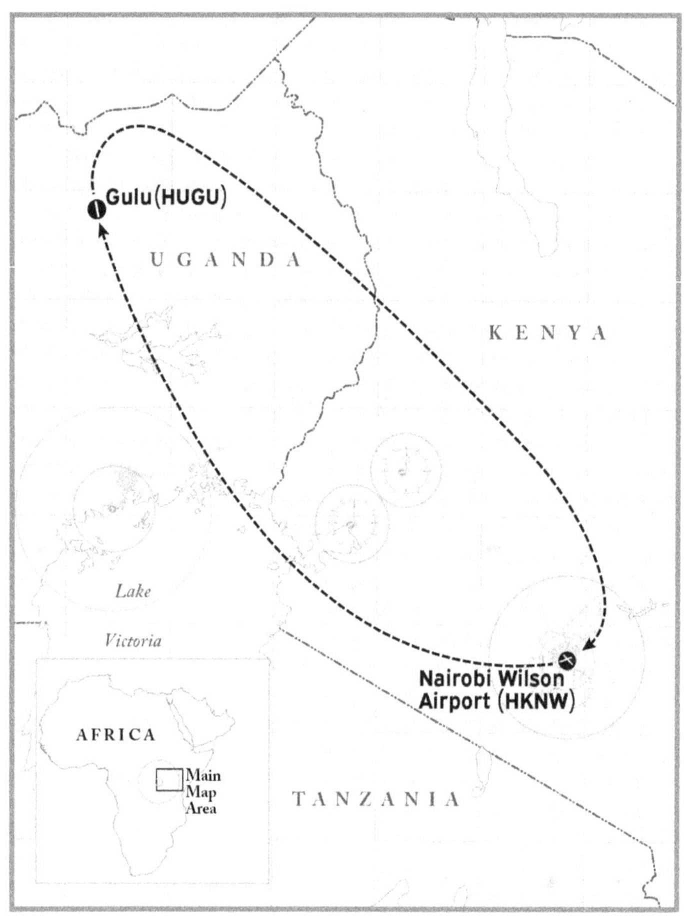

Flight to Gulu, Uganda, using a King Air

SANCTUARY

> *The atheist staring from his attic window is often nearer to God than the believer caught up in his own false image of God.*
>
> — Martin Buber

The dispatch center first called about the mission during dinner. It wasn't an interruption; I was alone at the Aero Club. I spent my evenings there reading the local papers and picking from an English menu that was a leftover from a time well before independence. That night, the pretty young waitress, formal in her black uniform and leather shoes, brought me sausages and mash and mushed peas and then sat quietly at another table reading a tattered soft-cover novel. She couldn't leave until the dining room closed at nine. In fellowship, we flipped pages.

I took the call from my usual table where, like most nights, I was the only customer in a dimly lit corner of the safari-themed dining room. The dispatcher came on the line and said that we were leaving first thing in the morning. We were headed to Uganda.

The dispatchers never got the patient's full story or the details of his life before he arrived at the small village hospital. Nobody knew whether he had family, or even why he had traveled alone to such a strange place. Maybe it was a midlife reawaking. In any case, it was unclear how an Austrian in sandals, carrying a backpack and sporting a long beard, had ended up by himself in such a remote corner of western Uganda, so far from the usual tourist traps.

The Ugandan hospital said that he had been camping in the remote bush, close to the reserves and the animals, when he abruptly developed a headache and fever. He tried to rest and to treat himself with fever medication, but as he became more ill, he knew he needed to be seen by a doctor. He hastily arranged a ride from the bush to Gulu. From there, he found his way to the mission hospital a few kilometers away, in a small village called Lacor. I could only imagine the fear, nausea, and desperation he must have felt on that final ride through the Ugandan bush—and the relief he felt, too, when he arrived at St. Mary's and saw the clean floors and sense of order and calm. The doctor said when the man arrived at the front gate, he stumbled from the back seat of the car toward the emergency room clutching his passport. He had to be supported by the security guards because he was nearly unconscious. He was incoherent with fever.

The doctors immediately tested him for malaria, the obvious diagnosis in Africa. It's also a malady that is often misdiagnosed, because making a firm diagnosis of malaria is somewhat of an art. Even today, diagnosing malaria is usually done by looking for specific parasites under a microscope. It's a simple test—smears of blood on a slide stained with a dye. Nevertheless, it takes skill to read the samples well. The lab technicians make two slides: one has a thick sample of the patient's blood so the technicians can scan a large number of cells quickly for rare parasites, and the other has a thin sample of blood to confirm the diagnosis and focus closely on the invaders. In the Austrian's case, the thick smear wasn't needed; there was no nuance. It was malaria. On the thin smear, the parasites were so plentiful that they filled the sample. They were actively invading his red blood cells, replicating, and invading yet more blood cells.

It was an overwhelming infection—among the worst the doctors had seen. They could tell by the patient's behavior and exam findings that he had a feared complication: he was suffering from cerebral malaria. The infection had caused inflammation of the linings of his brain and, ultimately, brain damage. One mosquito, a simple bite ten days earlier, had brought the Austrian to his knees.

Children and strangers to Africa are typically the two groups most vulnerable to severe cases of malaria. The reason is that neither has immunity. Unlike local children, though, the visitors usually take malaria prophylaxis to prevent infection. I had no idea whether the Austrian had taken a prophylaxis; but I knew his infection was killing him. The parasites were digesting his red blood cells. His kidneys were failing. The tissues in his lungs had become severely inflamed, leaving him struggling to breathe. The doctors urgently placed him on a ventilator, hoping to allow time for the intravenous quinine they were giving him to poison the parasites. It was a treatment hundreds of years old. But it wasn't enough. Having seen no improvement in the patient's condition, the hospital had called for a transport early in the morning.

We left in the twin-engine King Air for the three-hour flight west to Uganda. We needed to include a stop at the international airport in Entebbe, a city outside the capital of Kampala in central Uganda, so that the Ugandan military could give us official clearance to land at the airstrip in Gulu. This was unusual; the Ugandans knew Flying Doctors well, and we typically didn't need to stop in the capital when flying into the country. But Gulu had a legacy that made the authorities deeply uneasy. Gulu, in the northern and western part of Uganda, up near the South Sudanese border, had been home to rebels from the Lord's Resistance Army (LRA), which had waged war against the Ugandan government for twenty years.

The LRA was, by any global or historic measure, an extraordinarily ugly organization. The group's leader, a psychopath named Joseph Kony, dropped out of school at a young age and claimed to be a spirit medium and Christian freedom fighter. He spent years attempting to overthrow the government, to replace it with a theocracy based on his distorted views of the Ten Commandments. The group was an offshoot of earlier rebel groups which had arisen in the 1980s to defend Northern Uganda against attacks by the ethnically and culturally distinct Southern Uganda. The battle between the LRA and the government resulted in a massive displacement of Northern Ugandans—with nearly the entire Northern Ugandan population living, at one point, in hundreds of internally-displaced person camps in northern Uganda.

It was a difficult time to be traveling in Northern Uganda. The Ugandan government and the LRA had signed a truce in 2006; it was agreed that LRA forces would leave Uganda for the northern part of the Democratic Republic of Congo—and that the Ugandan government would not attack them as they did so. But, around the same time as we were headed to Gulu, the armed forces of Uganda, Congo, and South Sudan, all of whom were supported by the Americans who provided intelligence and logistics, raided the LRA camps in Congo, destroying most of them. The LRA would soon retaliate with attacks across the region.

It would be hard to overstate the evil that was done by the LRA. Each depravity was worse than the next. They perpetrated mass rapes and large-scale abductions of children, whom they turned into dead-eyed LRA child soldiers. These kids, victims of the LRA's "crimes against humanity" themselves, then began committing their own crimes against humanity. On Sundays, the child soldiers would sit in the streets looking for Ugandans who had violated the sabbath. Anyone found doing errands on Sundays would have their hands and legs chopped off with machetes. Their brutality was savagely violent.

To escape being abducted or murdered, every night, Ugandan children—all between the ages of three and seventeen—would flee their internally displaced person camps and seek shelter from the LRA in larger towns. There were estimated to be more than fifty thousand of these "night commuters."

Some of them would spend nights behind the walls of St. Mary's Hospital, where we were headed. The hospital would open its gates at dusk, and thousands of women and children would enter and find space to sleep on the hard ground outside the hospital. The guards would lock the tall gates until morning and then open them again, and the children would walk back to the camps.

St. Mary's was founded in 1959 by Italian Catholic missionaries. It started as a small thirty-bed dispensary. Over time, through international fundraising, it grew into a 500-bed hospital. When we visited, St. Mary's, along with its satellite clinics, served hundreds of thousands of patients a year. The main campus was a collection of simple metal-roofed buildings arranged around a plaza and surrounded by a tall wall that had been erected for protection against gunfire.

St. Mary's was no ordinary hospital; it had a distinguished history. In 1961, a physician couple, Dr. Lucille Teasdale and Dr. Piero Corti, arrived in Gulu to work at the small dispensary run by nuns. Together, they grew that institution into something more meaningful, significant, and lifesaving for the community. Teasdale was a woman ahead of her time. The daughter of a Montreal grocer, she had committed herself to becoming a doctor and missionary at the age of twelve. She later did her medical training at the University of Montreal, as one of only a few women students at that time, and ultimately became a pediatric surgeon.

She met Piero Corti, her eventual husband, in Quebec, where he was finishing his training in pediatrics. Corti was an Italian physician who also had planned at a young age to become a doctor working overseas. When they both completed their training, in 1961, the couple moved to the city of Gulu. Teasdale began work at St. Mary's as a surgeon, and Corti became the anesthesiologist and the radiologist. The two soon married in a ceremony that was witnessed by a dozen nuns in habit.

Despite enormous challenges, the hospital grew over the years, adding beds, training programs, and clinical capacity.

In 1982, the couple recruited an African physician, Dr. Matthew Lukwiya, to join them. Lukwiya was one of their early trainees and was a specialist in HIV. That same year, Dr. Teasdale began to lose weight and develop a series of unusual infections. She was diagnosed with HIV in 1985 and died of AIDS in 1996. She had accidentally cut herself during a surgery, probably sometime in the 1970s, long before anyone understood HIV. After her death, she was buried in the gardens of the hospital.

Dr. Lukwiya died soon after, in 2000, under extraordinary circumstances: an outbreak of Ebola, the largest ever recorded, flooded the hospitals of Gulu with hemorrhaging, highly infectious patients. After seeing two patients, Lukwiya clinically recognized the disease, instituted quarantine, alerted the CDC, and aggressively managed his patients' care. On one of the final days of the outbreak, while caring for a colleague, Lukwiya's eyes were splashed with blood. Fatigued, and in a hurry to help, he had forgotten to put on goggles. He died of Ebola hemorrhagic fever only a few days later. He was one of thirteen staff members who died of Ebola contracted from caring for patients at the hospital.

Dr. Corti worked for several years after his wife's death in 1996 but died of cancer in 2003. He is buried next to his wife and Dr. Lukwiya on the hospital grounds. All three devoted their entire professional careers to the hospital and to caring for members of the community.

Though the founders were no longer there, St. Mary's still operated with a remarkable level of professionalism, cleanliness, and order. When we arrived at the Gulu airstrip, we were met by a spotlessly clean Land Rover ambulance, which we loaded with ventilators, IV pumps, medication bags, IV fluids, and airway equipment. The driver began the five-kilometer drive down the rutted dirt roads to St. Mary's Hospital to collect the Austrian.

We had driven for several kilometers and were close to the hospital when John got a call: we could turn around, they said. We were too late. The Austrian had died only minutes ago. Not sure what to do, we continued on to the hospital. Once there, we got out of the truck, walked through the gates of the charity hospital without equipment, and headed to the small ICU. There, in a small corner, an exhausted anesthesiologist sat in sweaty scrubs. After days without sleep, fighting for the Austrian's life, the doctor looked like he was near tears.

At the other end of the six-bed ICU lay a gray corpse, a thin man in a hospital bed. Our Austrian. The nurses had washed him and combed his hair, and they had removed the tubes and lines that the anesthesiologist had inserted. They had covered his body in a clean white sheet and called for the priest. They all had put forth a valiant effort.

His was a lonely death. To be far from home, delirious but alert enough to desperately seek a hospital, knowing all the while that he'd made a fatal mistake, would have been devastating. He would've known he shouldn't have been by himself. He would've known he had waited too long to seek help.

I'm not religious; I've always been slightly skeptical of the pious. The evangelizing missionaries in Africa seem especially contemptible. We'd see them in airports across the continent: groups of sincere, middle-aged white people in identical T-shirts embossed with the name of some southern United States church and some slogan like "Repent Sinners: African Love Action and Reaction Trip 2002." There they'd sit, with their guitars and their moral smugness. I resented their simplistic earnestness, their deeply held convictions centered around their own superiority, and the calculating way they would offer some sort of token service—say, rebuilding a well or re-shingling an outhouse over a weekend—as an excuse to demonstrate their rectitude, and as justification for proselytizing to the Godless masses. Their perseverance and certitude seemed entirely self-serving.

Yet, the lives chosen by the three doctors who had run the impeccable Catholic hospital seemed to be something else entirely. In Uganda, standing in the St. Mary's ICU, I was struck by how religion could be a force for both good and evil. It could be co-opted by organizations like the LRA to oppress and injure millions. It could similarly be the justification for proselytization. And it could also be the impetus for a place like St. Mary's. Dr. Teasdale, Dr, Corti, and Dr. Lukwiya, all devout Catholics, had given their lives and all their gifts to the people of Gulu. They had led lives of service and humility—and they'd exemplified, almost to an unreasonable extreme, the highest aspirations of physician ethics. How much good had they done in their time?

Most people in the world want to live by a code. They want to have a set of beliefs and behaviors to aspire to, maybe a sense that there is a bigger purpose to it all. In my experience, most of the world's religions hold, at their cores, very similar precepts about how to live a decent life and care for others. What one learns over time, I think, is that humans are quite talented at validating extreme and sometimes extraordinarily inhumane actions in the name of a higher cause or the correcting of a perceived moral wrong. This has been especially true in Africa, a continent of popular uprisings and social movements, mass conversions, attempted theocracies, and genocide.

That afternoon, as we stood to the side in the small ICU, the anesthesiologist roused himself and then wandered off to try to call the embassy to track down family. The hospital would try to keep the body cool for a few days, too, until it could be repatriated. The others in the unit dispiritedly got back to work. They had 500 other beds to manage.

Outside, in the courtyard, tables that were set up under the covered porch of the hospital already had long lines of villagers registering to get help. An immensely pregnant woman was helped through the hospital's front gate. A tiny, crying baby was carried into the clinic by his mother. The death of the Austrian would be but only one of many that week. Almost certainly, hundreds more cases of malaria would arrive.

It was another normal day in the life of busy St. Mary's—a not-so-ordinary hospital with a distinguished and, to my mind, very special history.

John and I returned to the Land Rover dejectedly. The driver brought us back to the airstrip where the pilots were waiting. We loaded our equipment into the plane. Since we had unexpected free time, instead of boarding immediately, we decided to get a coffee and catch a bit of sun before takeoff.

On that beautiful morning at the Gulu airstrip, we pushed aside thoughts of the LRA and their perverted theology and tried not to think of the plights of the night commuters or the thousands and thousands of disembodied hands that had been sacrificed in the name of God. Instead, we surrounded ourselves with thoughts of the three doctors' unwavering commitment to the poor and the sick. Their vision of the world extended far outside of themselves. It added complexity and nuance to my own world view.

In time, the call to board came from the pilots. We climbed into the plane. The captain started the engines, and we took off into the wind. For the next three hours, we sat quietly, each alone with our thoughts. We'd be back in Nairobi in time for dinner.

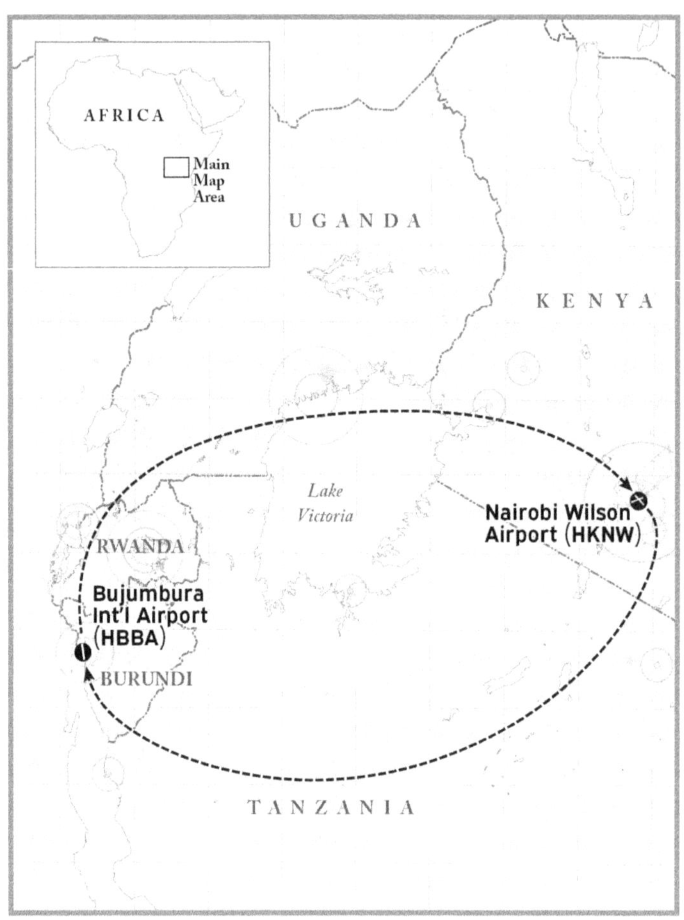

Evacuation from Bujumbura, Burundi, using a Citation

EXPLORERS

It is not all pleasure this exploration.

– David Livingstone

Just outside of Bujumbura, a city in Burundi on Lake Tanganyika, there is a big rock: the Livingstone Stanley Monument, which Burundians advertise—inaccurately, it turns out—as the place where explorer David Livingstone and journalist Henry Stanley first met in 1871.

Their story is well known. Dr. David Livingstone was a revered British explorer who, in 1866, set off on an expedition to locate the source of the Nile River. It was his most important expedition to date. But, months after arriving in Africa, all communication from Livingstone ceased. After several years with no word, many Europeans considered him dead.

In 1869, the brash editor of the *New York Herald* newspaper, in a plan to increase the paper's circulation (and to jab at the English, with whom the US had frosty relations) sent a journalist to find Livingstone—or at least his remains. The editor selected Henry Stanley, who was a swashbuckler but had no experience in Africa. Stanley was born British and came from humble origins in Wales, where he had been abandoned by his parents as a child. He reinvented himself in America as a Civil War soldier who fought for both the Union and Confederate armies. He later became a journalist.

Having never been in the tropics, the early part of Stanley's trip to Africa was a fiasco and almost killed him. While searching for Livingstone, Stanley battled cerebral malaria, starvation, and dysentery. One of his colleagues died from elephantiasis. The other died from smallpox. Undaunted, Stanley pursued Livingstone across the continent with single-minded determination.

Eventually, Stanley heard that a white man had been spotted in the town of Ujiji, near Lake Tanganyika. After traveling across the middle of Africa, from the islands of Zanzibar westward, he entered Ujiji in November 1871. There, he found a grizzled white man—one of the very few in Africa—confined to a hut in the Arab slave-trading village. It was Livingstone.

Livingstone's Nile expedition had collapsed years earlier. His supplies had been stolen, his team had died from fever, and his porters had deserted him. Tropical diseases had weakened him, too. Sick and poor, he had been forced to take up with Arab slave traders who were willing to house him but wouldn't let him communicate with the outside world.

Stanley liberated Livingstone, and the New York papers celebrated his discovery with front-page articles; the *Herald's* investment in Stanley's expedition had paid off. After regaining his strength, Livingstone continued his search for the head of the Nile, to no avail. Two years after being discovered by Stanley, he died from dysentery and malaria. Eventually, the head of the Nile would be found—by Stanley, who, after finding Livingstone in 1871, undertook several more expeditions in Africa. The source of the Nile was ultimately located in the mountains between Rwanda and Burundi.

These stories of early explorers of Africa are remarkable. Even in a time when supplies and communication were poor and medicine was nearly nonexistent, Stanley and Livingstone couldn't resist seeking riches, celebrity, and adventure in Africa—for better or worse.

A hundred and forty years later, I, too, found myself confronted with the perils that lay waiting for unknowing and unprepared travelers of Africa. That day, the victim of the deadly tropical diseases found on the shores of Lake Tanganyika was an aid worker from Germany. Remarkably, Africa had made such limited health care gains in those hundred and forty years that, a century and a half later, we were still treating the same diseases.

The airport terminal in Bujumbura was a series of peaked, igloo-like domes that looked like a line of Martian's helmets from a cartoon. Part Jetsons and part 1950s salon hairdryer, the airport's design reminded me that when Burundians gained independence in 1962, they had bold, futuristic goals for their country and wanted those goals reflected in their public architecture. As we taxied in across the rough tarmac, the slowly deteriorating airport buildings, stained by rain and mildew, were a sad testament to crushed ambitions.

From overhead, if one squinted just a little, Bujumbura resembled an old European city. There were neat grids of streets adjoining boulevards at obtuse angles; the commercial streets downtown had trees and roundabouts, offices buildings, and grand monuments to generals. But outside the core, the city quickly devolved into the right angles of tiny houses with rusting roofs, separated by mud streets; these were the shanties which housed the city's exploding population of 493,000 souls—the result of one of the world's highest fertility rates.

Poor and landlocked, the tiny German colony had been handed to the Belgians after World War I. Burundi had spent most of the years since independence enmeshed in civil war, ethnic cleansing, coups, massacres, and genocide. There had been no time to build an economy and no foundation upon which to build it. Since the 1960s, Burundi had been the world's poorest country when measured by GDP per capita. It was a collection of tiny dirt plots producing just enough food for its inhabitants.

We didn't have visas; we didn't need them for this trip. Our patient, an aid worker, would meet us after we landed. While we waited, we wandered alone through the secure areas of the Bujumbura airport. It was early in the day, and the lights in the terminal were still dark. The flight arrival and departure board was empty; later, there would be only a handful of regional flights that day—to Uganda, to Ethiopia, and to Kenya. Once a week, there was a flight to Brussels. The place felt exhausted, like it was cleaning up from a big party thrown years before. Peering through an unrolled screen barrier, I saw among the otherwise empty shelves of the sole duty-free shop about eight bottles of whiskey, a few cartons of cheap cigarettes, and a few bottles of what was advertised as Polo cologne for sale.

Our patient arrived on time at the front doors of the terminal, we could see her through the glass barriers. She was a friendly, but no-nonsense German woman in her thirties—a career aid worker, who, accompanied by colleagues from their NGO, had taken a taxi to the airport. Her hair was pulled back, and she wore the aid worker uniform of shapeless linen and cotton clothes in nondescript beiges and grays with locally made sandals. She hugged her friends goodbye and, using a cane, dragged herself and her bag through the token security check and met us in the terminal.

Dozens of aid workers had been my patients at Flying Doctors. They were an unusual bunch. In the scheme of things, they were doing God's work; they were men and women who were often so enmeshed in their missions that they were immune to the privations of the bush. Many were explorers in the Livingstone vein.

They had a mission, certainly, but they also very much sought freedom, risk, and adventure, and perhaps the power to allocate badly needed resources while making powerful decisions. Plenty of people have tried to make a difference in the world; only a self-declared sliver of them ended up in tents in Burundi.

The price for living this life of adventure and purpose was medical risk. For centuries, the developing world had been a treacherous place. Long-term visitors often became victims, both as a function of the time they spent exposed to illnesses in tropical Africa and the precautions they dropped through complacency. The biggest risk they all faced was infection.

East Africa's menagerie of infections—be they from viruses, bacteria, fungi, or parasites—could attack humans doing even the most routine activities. It had been that way for generations. Swimming in fresh water could infect you with bacterial illnesses and Schistosomiasis, a serious worm infection in which juvenile worms, called cercariae, easily entered through skin. Dysentery, which came from eating and drinking food contaminated with viruses and bacteria, including diseases such as Typhoid and Shigella, was a deadly risk. Unprocessed milk could be lethal. Breathing could expose you to tuberculosis.

But that list barely scratched the surface. Vector-borne illnesses included viruses, bacteria, and parasites carried by insects such as tsetse flies (whose bites could cause African sleeping sickness) and mosquitos (which carried dozens of illnesses, including malaria). Plus, there were fleas and ticks and lice. And then there were the sexually transmitted infections, which went beyond the usual suspects to include painful ulcers called chancroid and masses called Granuloma Inguinale. Just existing in rural Africa required vigilance.

And so it went with our patient. She'd been in Africa for years. In the plane, she told me that, over a period of weeks, she had developed a large swelling of her upper thigh, and a few weeks later the swelling grew to include her entire leg. Her leg was warm to the touch and had swollen to twice its normal size. The local doctors worried that she had a deep vein thrombosis—blood clots in the veins of the lower leg—but without an ultrasound, they couldn't be sure. If they were right, this was an emergency. Without blood thinners, the clots could break off and travel to her lungs. If big enough, the clots could kill her.

But I wasn't sure that her presumptive diagnosis was right. I inspected the patient as she lay back, looking closely at her leg. Her legs were asymmetrical. The affected leg *was* swollen, but when I pushed on her calf and her skin dented inward, creating a divot, she had no pain. A blood clot typically causes tenderness in the calf when squeezed. Instead, the lymph nodes of her groin were inflamed and tender and sore. I'd seen these symptoms before—in a textbook of tropical disease. I suspected it was filariasis, the same disease that had killed Stanley's colleague.

Filariasis is a parasitic disease. To catch it, you must be bitten by a mosquito that has injected tiny worms (microfilaria) into your skin. These develop into worm-like parasites that are between four and ten centimeters long. They clog the lymphatic system and prevent the fluid in tissues from being reabsorbed. Our patient told me that she had been bitten by a lot of mosquitos in the rural area where she lived, but that she had been careful to take her malaria tablets. That story fit: the malaria tablets wouldn't work to prevent filariasis. If not treated, one could die. Or, over a course of years, the leg might remain permanently swollen. When that happens, the skin thickens (like that of an elephant), and one is left with lifelong elephantiasis. The treatment these days is relatively easy: anti-parasitic medication. In Livingstone's era, there was no treatment. You'd see these unfortunate souls, brought from the tropical colonies, working as circus and sideshow performers.

Adventure. It's a dangerous drug. I thought about what had brought Livingstone and Stanley to Africa—and what had made them stay, even as they grew ill with multiple infections, some of which brought them close to death. What was their intense perseverance about? Was Stanley seeking fame to compensate for his humble origins? Was Livingstone seeking national adulation at a time when explorers were like today's movie stars? What possessed Livingstone to refuse rescue and repatriation to continue his search for the Nile? His adamance led only to his death. Why did Stanley continue Livingstone's search for the source of the White Nile? He lost hundreds of men in the process.

It had been 140 years since Livingstone and Stanley dragged themselves across the African Savanna, each seriously ill with tropical diseases. And here we were, making identical diagnoses in the same spot. Public health interventions had eradicated *some* of these diseases—ones that also used to exist in the West. For example, in 1935, there were a hundred thousand cases of malaria in the United States. Precursor organizations to today's

Centers for Disease Control were created to eradicate the disease; through a program of malaria treatment and mosquito eradication, malaria was eliminated in the US in 1951. But clean water, sewage systems, vector control, access to therapies, and public education—although all basic and cost effective—were grindingly hard to accomplish in East Africa. The reasons were complex. Money was certainly an issue. But logistics, access to labs, geography, and factors such as insecticide resistance were also problems. So, we were still treating dysentery, malaria, and lymphatic filariasis in explorers in Africa.

The diagnosis of filariasis had advanced much over the years since Stanley's men had died of it. It's still diagnosed under a microscope, usually in the dark. Since mosquitos bite mainly at night, the parasites and their mosquito carriers have developed a fascinating symbiosis: the microfilaria come out when the mosquitos bite. They hide out in your lungs during the day, and then enter your bloodstream at night where they can be sucked back into a hungry mosquito for transmission to the next person. Nurses, fortunately, have also evolved to suck blood from humans at night. To get a sample of blood with a high likelihood of containing the nocturnal microfilaria, they set their alarms for midnight blood collections.

There now were accurate antigen tests available, too; and under ultrasound, the worms can be seen moving around in the lymph system, doing something called the "filarial dance." In all likelihood, the nurses at the private hospital in Nairobi who would treat this patient would be up at midnight drawing samples to be put under the microscope. If the diagnosis I made was found to be correct, our young aid worker would receive fistfuls of medicine to kill the filaria.

We didn't have much to do on the flight to Nairobi. Our patient was chatty and made friends easily, typical for NGO workers and military folks posted overseas. So, we chatted about aid work and starvation in Burundi, and the challenges and rewards of being an aid worker in Africa. The leg was bad news, she said. But as soon as she healed up, she'd be back.

She couldn't stay away.

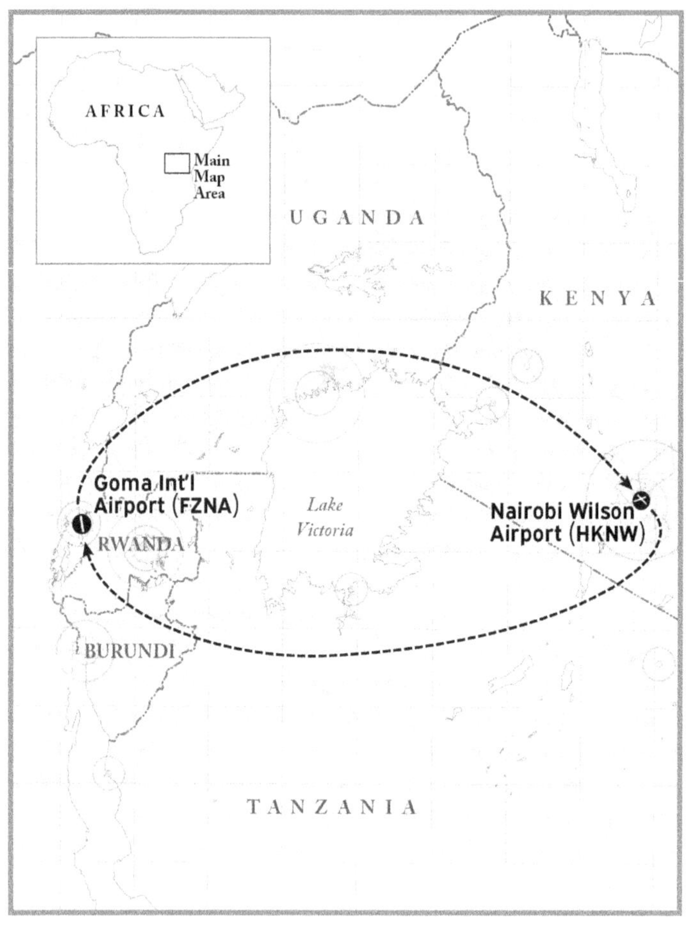

Evacuation from Goma, DRC, using a Citation

DIVINE INTERVENTION

Turning and turning in the widening gyre
The falcon cannot hear the falconer;
Things fall apart; the centre cannot hold;
Mere anarchy is loosed upon the world,
The blood-dimmed tide is loosed, and every-where
The ceremony of innocence is drowned;
The best lack all conviction, while the worst
Are full of passionate intensity.

— WB Yeats

Goma is a once-lovely and now sad sweaty city that sits in the eastern part of the vast Democratic Republic of Congo (DRC), not far from the border with Rwanda. It's an unlucky place, starting with its inauspicious location on the slope of a volcano, Nyiragongo, which regurgitates lava that buries the city and the airport runway every few years. The city also sits next to Lake Kivu, which, though picturesque (even when seen through the typical haze of burning garbage), is a bomb waiting to go off: the lake is apparently due for a "limnic eruption," whereby massive quantities of volcanic methane and CO2 are released from the lake's depths, rising to the surface and smothering everyone for miles. Periodically, the lake belches a *mazuku* (Swahili for "evil wind"), a smaller pocket of carbon dioxide that can accumulate insidiously and, when released, smother people and livestock. There was a similar limnic eruption in 1986, at a volcanic lake in Cameroon. There, carbon dioxide under pressure descended into nearby villages, killing 1,700 people.

But, in Goma, as with Congo in general, the biggest problems have been man-made. Since 1994, Goma has been at the center of Africa's most significant wars.

The DRC's host of problems in 2012 (grave human rights abuses, atrocities committed against civilians, conflicts between the numerous armed militias, and international conflicts with Rwanda and Uganda) first began outside its borders— specifically, in Rwanda.

Rwanda sits immediately next to Goma; in fact, it's only a few hundred feet due east of Goma's airport. The Rwandan civil war began as a tribal war between two clans: the Hutu and the Tutsi. The Hutu represented 85 percent of the population, and the minority Tutsi represented 15 percent of the population. Historians argue that European colonists in Rwanda promoted minority Tutsi interests—economically, politically, and legally— over those of the Hutu, as a matter of policy.

Eventually, the majority Hutu rose, and the once-powerful Tutsi were forced to flee Rwanda. A vicious civil war erupted in the 1980s, as rebel Tutsi groups launched attacks against Rwandan Hutu. There were ultimately peace negotiations and plans for a transitional government, and the UN set up a peacekeeping operation in 1993. Then, in 1994, the powder keg was lit. In April of that year, the Rwandan president's plane was shot down. This event led to a power vacuum and an uprising against the moderate successors to the president. Genocidal killings, born of a planned Hutu plot to finally eliminate the Tutsi, broke out. What resulted was one of the worst examples of genocide in modern history. The goal was to kill every Tutsi in Rwanda. Over 500,000 died, often by machete. The policy of ethnic identity cards, which facilitated the genocide, had originally been imposed by the Germans who controlled Rwanda after World War I and was continued after they left.

A flood of Rwandans, over one and a half million people, left for DRC—which was, at that point, called Zaire. The Rwandan fight spilled into Zaire, especially Eastern Zaire, and rebels launched attacks and counter attacks from Eastern Zaire, outside Goma. Rwanda eventually invaded Zaire to fight the rebels who were based there. This fighting turned into the First Congo War, which ultimately led to the collapse of the Zairian government, then led by longtime despot Mobutu Sese Seko. This, in turn, led to the formation of a new Zairian government under the rebel Laurent Kabila. The country was renamed the Democratic Republic of Congo.

After a short period of rest, in 1998, the Second Congo War began in the now newly named Democratic Republic of Congo. It revolved around similar issues as the first war, but it also now involved interests from across the African continent. In 2002, after four long years of war, a peace agreement was finally signed. Sporadic violence, however, continued to occur in eastern DRC.

The truce was extremely uneasy: The United Nations Mission in the Democratic Republic of Congo (MONUC) was established by the UN Security Council to monitor the peace process following the Second Congo War. A peacekeeping force, the UN's largest—ultimately numbering sixteen thousand troops from dozens of countries—was installed with very specific mandates that limited what they could do militarily: they were there to secure the airport and protect both refugees and civilians.

East DRC was still super-hot; rebels regularly attacked MONUC soldiers, and civilians rioted, demanding better protection from the UN. Within a few months of our arrival in Goma, in 2012, war would again break out in the city, now between Tutsi militia backed by Rwanda, and the DRC army backed by MONUC. The rebels would ultimately capture Goma and its surrounding area in a battle that caused a widespread humanitarian crisis. By 2012, NGOs would claim that the wars in what is now known as the Democratic Republic of Congo, which had begun in 1996, had led to more deaths than any conflict since World War II. Around six million lives were lost, not including the estimated 500 thousand to 800 thousand deaths from the Rwandan genocides that occurred prior to 1996.

It was against this backdrop that we were called to Goma on one bright morning. At seven, we took off from Wilson bound for Goma's airport. We were headed there to pluck out a sick priest. Nobody on the plane was thrilled; aside from the basic dangers of flying an unarmed civilian plane into a conflict zone (which Goma still was), the city was notoriously corrupt. We all knew that we would be shaken down every minute we were on the ground. The captain told me that the Goma airport was a place requiring any number of "green forms." In Africa, you were required to fill out blue, white, and pink forms. But someone would inevitably ask you for the "green form," as well. A handful of US dollars would be handed over in exchange for a sneer or toothy grin. I was warned that once we touched down, the tarmac would be swarmed with form collectors of every ilk: fuel guys, paperwork guys, wheel chock guys, ministry guys, squeegee guys. No matter how sick the patient, or urgent the departure, these guys would sit on the retractable stairs of the plane and refuse to get off until paid.

As far as they were concerned, Santa's sleigh had arrived in the form of our AMREF plane. The pilots claimed that this degree of petty corruption was a national characteristic in Congo, worse than most other

African countries and modeled by Mobutu, who himself had seized private assets in the 1970s for distribution to his "Big Vegetable" loyalists. It now permeated every transaction.

While on our approach, we could hear and feel the landing gear being lowered and engaged. From the air, the airport looked like a fortress: white UN tanks and armored personnel carriers sat maybe every twenty feet along the runway. Tall earthen walls ran the length of the runway, to protect from snipers. Sentries and heavy artillery covered every plane coming and going. Most of the planes were massive white UN cargo flights traveling in convoys. Our small plane was a curiosity.

We landed and taxied to the tarmac next to UN transport planes. A ground agent guided us in with batons; soon, the engines spun down. We all sighed in resignation. Let the onslaught begin. The captain opened our side door with a whoosh. As the stairs fell, I had my first look at Goma. The airport was low-slung and gray. The air was hazy and smelled of acrid smoke. In the distance stood a bunch of workers in reflective vests. We prepared to be eaten alive.

And…nothing.

This time, we sat alone. Nobody approached the

door, except for a short man who placed chocks on our wheels and left. Shocked, I climbed out and stood next to the wing. Then, through the haze, I saw an apparition that wasn't: it was a solid man wearing a spotless white vestment, starched collar, and dress shoes. He carried a two-pound crucifix, which hung on a gold chain around his neck. The chain swung as he moved with a quick and purposeful stride across the tarmac toward the plane. Conscious of my sweaty uniform shirt and dusty boots, I stared as he walked over alone. He introduced himself as the Bishop of Goma.

The bishop was larger than life and utterly confident. With a big smile, he grabbed my hand and rested his other hand on my arm, and then he greeted the pilots and Kione, our nurse on this trip.

Bienvenue, he said. He gestured around. "It's too bad," he said, looking dismissively at the troops and the ramshackle huts that climbed up the slopes of Mount Nyiragongo. "*Les temps sont difficiles*..."

I hadn't spoken French in decades, not since high school, and I was painfully aware of my inelegant accent. Alas, I was to be the sole linguist on this trip. Kione, having been the Swahili translator during every other trip we had taken together, looked at me with perhaps a measure of newfound respect.

The bishop and I quickly got down to business. A priest from the diocese was on his way to the airport and was quite ill. The health care in Goma was extremely limited. The ambulance would be there shortly. We were to do God's work.

I noticed, as we stood chatting, that the ground staff had stayed far away. When one approached the plane door to complete one task or another, he would almost genuflect and avert his eyes. The pilots stared incredulously, eyes alternating between the workers near the hangars and the three of us having an uninterrupted catch-up. They had never, in all their years in Goma, not been shaken down by this point in the visit, and they watched silently as the airport functioned as an airport should.

The bishop was serene and wise, an island of peace in the midst of chaos. He confidently asserted himself, gesturing with his hands at the gaggle of workers on the periphery to get them to make way for a van which came toward the plane, turned, and then backed toward us.

An assistant jumped from the passenger seat and lifted the rear hatch. Inside the ancient cargo van sat a nun wearing a plain skirt and blouse from the 1950s, thick stockings, and a veil; and three concerned aides who each seemed to be near panic. On the floor between them, lying on a dirty mattress, was a middle-aged, quite ashen priest gasping for air.

Kione and I jumped into the ambulance and lifted up the priest, who was in pajamas and covered in damp sweat. The bishop looked past the van and gestured to some of the rubberneckers in reflective vests. They skittered over to help support the priest and lift him onto the plane.

Kione and I quickly got to work. Lying on a stretcher in the plane, the priest had closed his eyes. He *was* sick, very sick, probably a major heart attack. He was Italian and spoke good English. Kione and I listened to his story as we started IVs and tried to get the EKG pads to stick to his sweaty chest. In the middle of the night, he'd had severe tearing pain in his chest and back. The diocese had taken him to the regional hospital, which had called AMREF.

I worried that our patient was either currently in the midst of his heart attack or had had an aortic dissection, where the walls of the main artery in the chest split open. Both diagnoses were bad, and they could be hard to distinguish without testing—typically, via an ultrasound or a CT. All we could do on the tarmac was obtain an EKG to look for signs of a large coronary artery obstruction and do a series of physical exams which might point to a dissection. Big differences are suggestive of a dissection, so we would check blood pressure on one arm and then the other. But that was an almost academic exercise; the sensitivity of physical exams was low. Kione got an EKG, which showed that the priest's heart was irritable and had signs that it wasn't receiving enough oxygen. It was a nondiagnostic finding.

We took stock: the priest's blood pressure was acceptable, and his pain was better after medication. We needed to bug out. Waiting for a dissection or heart attack to worsen was foolish.

The copilot was working the radios for clearance. The bishop, in his impeccable white vestments, peered through the door as the priest waved a feeble goodbye. The bishop gazed at me and then gestured to the nun who was already belted in, sitting with perfect posture in her seat toward the back.

"Docteur," he said. *"Elle apporte l'argent."* She brought the money.

The nun looked at us, reached into her modest handbag, and pulled out a thick envelope of cash secured with elastic bands—US dollars—to cover medical costs and the evacuation. It was somehow incongruous. I would maybe have been less surprised if she had pulled out a pistol. But, of course, this would all be expensive. It's not as if personal checks and health insurance plans were accepted in the DRC. Neither Kione nor I had any interest in bill collection; we wouldn't know where to begin. The bishop gestured to her to put the money back in her bag.

The priest's aides—who, it turned out, maintained the seminary and priest's accommodations—made tearful goodbyes and several signs of the cross, and then they stood next to the plane, craning to look through the window and the still-open door to get any news from the blip on the EKG monitor.

Outside the plane, there was a whole scene taking place. Grown women filed by the plane exchanging pleasantries and curtsying and giggling. For their part, the ground staff worked more diligently than ever before—to fuel the plane, to close the stairs, and to prepare to wave us off the tarmac. This, too, according to the pilots, had never happened before. Perhaps too awed by the bishop, or too embarrassed to be seen by him demanding bribes, no ground workers demanded a green form. Not one.

The workers' behavior was astonishing on the one hand, but it felt performative on the other. These were people who would gladly extort an air ambulance most days. But here, in front of the bishop, they genuflected and maintained a studious piousness. To me, it felt like bullshit: hypocrisy of the highest order. Yet, as we worked on the priest, I suddenly realized how easy it was for me, lacking any real information or context, to judge my surroundings. What was true was that Goma and its people and their customs required observation and empathy, and a perspective measured in generations. It was far too easy, in my position of undisputed authority, to punch down. There was a long history of the Catholic church in Congo. And Congo's problems had begun well before the Rwandan tribal wars.

One hundred years earlier, the land where we now stood had been privately owned by one man: Belgian King Leopold II. In the 1880s, Leopold had convinced European governments that he was providing humanitarian work in Congo. As a reward for his work, and for his promise not to tax trade in the region, King Leopold was ultimately named as the personal owner of Congo Free State. It was a massive area—over a million square miles—and was his alone. The land was a personal project; it was not gifted to him under his purview as King of Belgium, but to Leopold the humanitarian.

Leopold engaged Henry Morton Stanley, who, five years after his adventure with Livingstone, was still conveniently an explorer for hire. Leopold sent Stanley to solidify Leopold's grip on the region. Carrying out the king's order, Stanley established treaties with the local leaders that gave land rights to Leopold. Then, using a force of white mercenary officers and black soldiers, Leopold extracted a fortune in ivory and natural rubber from the Congo. In some cases, he awarded concessions to companies, giving them exclusive geographies. The invention of the inflatable tire led to a rapid increase in brutality in the Congo. The explosive demand for rubber required forced labor to optimize profits. Villagers who refused to participate in rubber collection or who failed to meet the required quotas could be killed or lose a hand. Estimates suggest that ten million Congolese died during King Leopold's command of the Free State of Congo (1885–1908). They died from murder, disease, or being worked to death.

The Abir Congo Company was a notorious rubber concessionaire. Leopold had awarded the company a lucrative area, and Abir had imposed a rubber quota on the men in the concession's villages. This quota was enforced by sentries who ensured production goals were met. The penalty for any man not meeting his quota was imprisonment of the man's family; the men, of course, were needed as workers.

The degree of violence, ruthlessness, and greed in Congo was the basis for Joseph Conrad's *Heart of Darkness*. Conrad was a merchant mariner who, in 1890, was hired by a Belgian trading company to work on one of its ships. Conrad ultimately piloted the ship up the Congo River to the company's innermost trading station. The horrors of what he saw on the trip had served as inspiration for his novel, which was (and still is) seen by many readers as a bleak repudiation of colonialism.

Christian missionaries working in the Congo were appalled by the mistreatment and abuse of the Congolese, and they raised international outrage. Alice Seeley Harris was an English missionary who photographed tortured Congolese during her visits to the Congo Free State at the turn of the century. In one famous photo, taken in 1904, Harris captured a man in mourning. His family had been attacked by sentries from the Abir company after he had failed to generate his rubber quota. The man, named Nsala, was holding a nest of leaves in which had been placed the severed hand and foot of his murdered five-year-old daughter. It is a devastating image.

By 1908, the missionaries, highlighting the atrocities in the Congo on road shows in Europe and America, had created sufficient international pressure that Leopold was forced to give his holdings to the Belgian Government. After twenty-three years, the Congo Free State became the Belgian Congo. It would remain a colony of Belgium until 1960.

Yet, perhaps inadvertently, the Belgian takeover of Congo put the Catholic Church in a powerful position. Several historians consider Belgium to have been an "appalling" colonial power, though of course the bar was quite low. Belgium itself was a young, fractured country. They were late coming to Africa and had limited experience administering lands far from Europe. In Congo, as in Ruanda-Urundi (which became Rwanda and Burundi in 1962), Belgians promoted the concept of the "colonial trinity" *(trinité coloniale)* of state, missionary, and private company interests—including those, obviously, of the Catholic Church.

With state sponsorship and support, the Church went on to develop schools and hospitals throughout the Congo. The Protestant missions were not as strongly supported, but they also grew. In 2008, the DRC was 96 percent Christian, around half of which were Catholic. For almost a century, the Catholic Church consistently provided the bulk of the country's elementary education and much of its health care.

As with many African countries, Congolese independence proved not to be a panacea. The Belgians left abruptly in 1960. After achieving independence, Congo then entered a sixty-year period in which the country vacillated between abusive dictatorships, secessionist movements, and a series of wars which caused the deaths of millions of Congolese. What remained constant over those sixty years of corruption and bloodshed was the presence of the Catholic Church.

The workers on the tarmac, I realized, had known nothing but ineffective governance from their government. But they knew the Church as the sole functioning institution in an otherwise bleak and corrupt political landscape. From the earliest days, the Church had formed a parallel structure to compensate for the vicissitudes of failed government and narrow-minded tribal conflicts. It intervened when it needed to, protested when it had to, and steadfastly built basic human services. It was, for a population starving for decency, something to hold onto and to respect. The genuflections of the ground staff weren't performative. The priest and his crucifix, and his church's relative decency, were everything to these people. My cynicism was unmerited. I was in no position to judge their sense of the sacred.

Anxious to get the priest into a hospital, I was relieved when we were ready to go. I took a last look at the decrepit shacks beyond the earthen fence and thought of the failed kleptocratic government and the UN, which continued to try to maintain order.

Congo seemed cursed by its own history. How could the DRC be functional after generations of greed and brutality? How could the place meaningfully move forward with the brutal scars of the past hundred years? How would the endless ethnic fights between Hutu and Tutsi be resolved? How did one live with the dismemberment of one's five-year-old-daughter, while questioning whether you were responsible for her death because you hadn't met a rubber production quota? History was destiny.

Our priest seemed to be in better shape, less ashen. The medications we had given him were helping. Joseph would meet us in Nairobi, and the Nairobi hospital would be ready with a cardiac cath lab and imaging when we arrived.

With the nun and her remarkable handbag strapped in, the pilots shut the door of the Citation and started the engines. There were no green bills to pay, nobody sitting on the plane steps. Except for the man guiding our departure, all the ground workers had clustered around the bishop on the far end of the parking area. The jet's lights flicked on and off like usual, and then cool air-conditioning from the ceiling created a jet of fog.

I could smell the kerosene and exhaust as the engines came to life. They were comforting reminders that we were leaving. Yet, it was also true that I was exactly where I wanted to be. The intensity of our focus, our impeccable planning and execution, and our clever medicine had outmaneuvered death. I felt in flow, consumed by the moment, so engaged that I lost track of time. The dangers of this trip were highly ill-advised. But, if I were to dig a bit, I'd admit that the ambiguity, the darkness, and the chaos all felt very familiar to me. Sometimes, I'd seek them, be drawn to these awful situations. I felt that I had experienced this type of darkness before and knew how to navigate it intuitively, as if I were well-equipped to enter these depths.

We taxied past the UN helicopters and planes, past the slums at the end of the runway, past the African soldiers with their ill-fitting uniforms and their Kalashnikovs, and past the thin, idle civilians sitting on the barricades staring at the planes. We turned onto the runway.

With white UN tanks marking the far edges of the runway, we accelerated, leaving Goma behind. I peered back at the van, looking for the bishop on the tarmac, wondering if he would still be there providing blessings and prayers, and if the crowd of ground workers would still be clustered around him and the seminarians. But as we climbed and headed toward the dense jungle, he was gone, like an apparition.

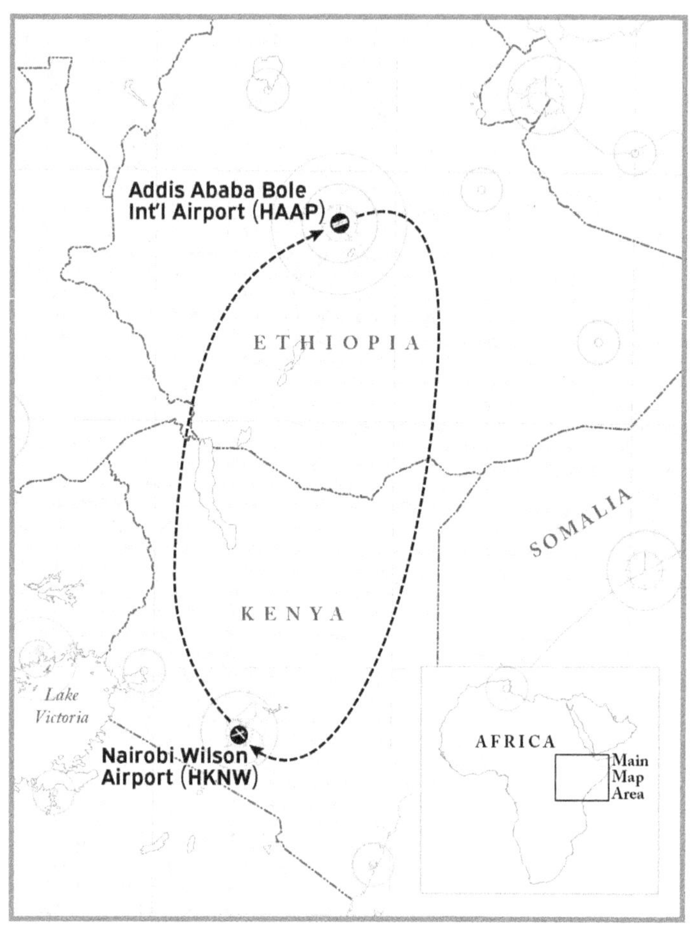

Evacuation from Addis Ababa, Ethiopia, using a Citation

FEVER

> *To mess around with Ebola is an easy way to die. Better to work with something safer, such as anthrax.*
>
> – Richard Preston, *The Hot Zone*

The Spaniard looked like he was from central casting: a young explorer with dark wavy hair, a pack of cigarettes in his front pocket, and a voluble dislike for any form of bureaucracy. He was traveling Africa alone. Before his eyes had sunk into his skull and his skin had turned yellow, I bet he'd been a real James Dean.

After being sick for ten days, the Spaniard had presented at a clinic outside Addis Ababa, Ethiopia. He had tried to manage his illness alone, in his hotel, taking fluids and fever medications. But by the time he arrived at the clinic, he was undeniably ill. Along with the fever, he had developed a headache, neck stiffness, muscle pain, and weakness. These were all signs of a bad infection, of a body reacting violently to an intrusion. Figuring out which infection he had would be the trick. The right diagnosis was essential. Each antibiotic covered a different type of intruder. Get the wrong one, and the patient slips even more deeply into sickness.

The clinic in Addis was accustomed to fever work-ups; they'd done thousands. So, they started all the usual tests, including bloodwork for the most important suspect: malaria. Malaria was all over East Africa. Over millennia, it had changed history and entire geographies; it had caused swamps to be drained and cities to be abandoned. Though it had been driven from the northern hemisphere, it persevered as the most significant tropical infection in poor places in the global South. Malaria was an African scourge; it drained productivity and caused misery and death.

There is a certain elegance to the malaria parasite, which is called Plasmodium. The bite of an infected mosquito injects into its human meal the mosquito's saliva, which is filled with an embryonic form of the parasite. These are called sporozoites. The sporozoites immediately head for the human liver, where they invade liver cells and grow into more mature forms, called merozoites. The merozoites are then released to attack and invade red blood cells, sometimes growing to a massive number.

Some malarial parasites will develop inside the human body into sexual forms, called gametocytes. These gametocytes are ready to be sucked up by the next mosquito who stops to feed. Inside the mosquito's body, these gametocytes come together and develop into oocysts, or egg forms. The oocysts then produce more sporozoites, which are injected into another unsuspecting human. It kicks off a next cycle of infection and misery. Malaria can quickly kill newcomers, foreigners, who have no immunity; the same is true for African children.

But, in a weird diagnostic twist, the doctors could find no malaria in the Spaniard. They peered at blood cells under a microscope, looking at thick and thin smears of stained blood, and found nothing. Worried that they somehow had missed seeing the telltale signs of malaria—the microscope diagnosis was notoriously fickle and operator- dependent—they started empiric treatment for malaria, anyway. They also began antibiotics for typhoid fever, a bacterial illness caused by the ingestion of contaminated food and water.

But still, he didn't get better. Over the next couple of days, the Spaniard's condition only got worse. On day three, his liver stopped working; on day five, his nose began to bleed, spontaneously, dripping red waves across the sheets. He became severely anemic, and his fever became more pronounced: he would shake with chills, and then his fever would break. Nobody knew what he had.

Then his urine turned blood red.

That was when the clinic called us in. The Spaniard needed to be in a modern hospital. We'd met him in the back of an Ethiopian ambulance that was parked next to the plane on the tarmac at the Addis Ababa airport. I first spied him from a distance: a shrunken man lying on a thin stretcher. He was dehydrated, his eyes were sunken, and he was severely jaundiced from his failing liver. I lifted his wrist to measure his pulse and found a faint, fast cadence. His blood pressure was spotty.

Kione handed me the folder from the clinic. As I looked at the ballpoint pen-filled pages, I could see that almost every value was abnormal. His red cells had been destroyed, and his blood didn't clot properly; it was as thin as water. His liver was damaged, and his kidney function and electrolytes were all over the map.

To make good decisions, doctors need to be dispassionate. Be empathetic, sure, but stay removed from the personal entanglements. At the end of the day, of course, the doctor is not the one with the problem. Yet, unlike nearly every other specialty in medicine, infectious disease challenges our dispassionate voice. This is for two reasons. The first is that we know that we, too, are one mosquito bite away from disaster. The Spaniard reminded me that my age and recent arrival were no protections. My immune naivety was nothing but a detriment.

The second reason is that human-to-human, patient-to-doctor transmission was a real concern. Infectious diseases—tuberculosis, respiratory illnesses, many viruses— could be spread easily in the back of an ambulance. We were at risk in a way far different from when we treated heart attacks or cancer. These illnesses were deadly, and there was little we could do to prevent transmission.

I remembered a story I had read just that year. A woman, a Zambian travel agent, was living a simple life on a small farm on the outskirts of Lusaka. One August day, she dropped a glass bottle and cut her leg. A day or two later, she developed a severe headache—but she was able to pull herself together and fly to South Africa for a wedding. There, she developed chills and had to take breaks from dancing to warm herself at a fireplace. A few days later, back in Lusaka, she became more ill with fever, chest pain, a sore throat, and a rash.

Zambian doctors admitted her to a local hospital. There, she was placed on a ventilator. At some point, an air ambulance was called to bring her back to South Africa where she died in the hospital, with brain swelling, a failed liver, and bleeding caused by low platelets. Nobody knew what she had.

Unexpectedly, a week later, the paramedic who had treated the travel agent also became sick. He was admitted to the same hospital that she had been transferred to. He died a few days later. Then, a nurse who had cared for the woman also became ill and died. Then, a hospital cleaner. Then a second nurse, who survived after doctors realized that they were dealing with a hemorrhagic virus like Ebola and began antiviral therapy. Eventually, scientists discovered that it had been a new hemorrhagic virus in the Arenavirus family: the Lujo virus.

Standing on the tarmac, we had a tough decision

to make. We needed to decide whether we should, in fact, fly the Spaniard to Nairobi. He had a fever, a damaged liver, blood that wouldn't clot, and he was actively bleeding. There was no diagnosis from the Ethiopian hospital that we could rely on. If it were a hemorrhagic virus, he would die— and we likely would, as well. We would also bear the responsibility for having imported the disease into one of Africa's largest cities. It would be a catastrophic error in judgment.

The alternative, of course, in the absence of suitable biohazard isolation equipment, might be to leave the Spaniard in Ethiopia to die. We could pack him back in the hot ambulance and ship him back to the Ethiopian hospital, assuming there was still a bed to be had. It would be the most responsible medical decision from a perspective of maximizing good for the most people. But, of course, it would be a cost fully borne by the Spaniard.

There is no provision in the Hippocratic oath that allows a doctor to sacrifice a patient for the greater good. The Declaration of Geneva, written following the atrocities committed by German physicians in World War II, demands that the health and well-being of a doctor's patient, and respect for his autonomy and dignity, be the doctor's ultimate priorities. Yet, the Declaration also requires doctors to pledge themselves to the service of humanity—which, presumably, would include not unleashing a highly virulent virus on an unsuspecting city of five million people.

On the ground in Ethiopia, I realized that this tension between public health and patient autonomy had been caused by medical scarcity. It was a tension we didn't face in the US; there, we could both save our patient and protect the public due to the availability of isolation rooms, HEPA filters, transport Isolettes, and the like, which greatly reduced the likelihood of disease transmission—although, in fairness, viral hemorrhagic fevers were so unusual that they would tax even the US system, as they demand a higher level of isolation than most hospitals can provide. But I could think of no comparable medical analog. I could not think of any time in my medical training or career where I would be called to sacrifice a life to save the lives of an abstract population of strangers, my own life included. I was, ultimately, the Spaniard's doctor. My responsibility to him was absolute.

If our suspicion was high enough, we would need a way to protect ourselves and the public while not abandoning him. Was there a middle ground? Should

I stay in Ethiopia? I didn't know. Did actually meeting the Spaniard in person make my obligation greater than it would have been had we triaged and refused a flight in advance from Nairobi? My instincts said yes. The Spaniard had become my responsibility.

I loved working with Kione. He had joined AMREF as a full-time flight nurse about a year earlier, but he had years of hospital experience. He was older and carried himself with a certain detachment, dignity, and calm demeanor. He seemed impossible to fluster. After many flights together, I realized that Kione's tolerance for risk and ambiguity, having worked in Kenyan hospitals his entire career, was higher than mine. I looked at him and shared my concerns about transporting a hemorrhagic virus to Nairobi. What did he think we should do?

Kione approached my question deliberately, thoughtfully, and with the perspective of someone who had learned to take calculated risks in a different environment with a radically different risk profile than the one I understood. He would defer to my judgment, he said; but ultimately, fever was common, and a hemorrhagic virus in a new patient presenting to the ED was a daily risk he and his colleagues had dealt with for years. Providing health care in Africa was like that.

They operated without the safety nets—the protective equipment and advanced diagnostics and sterility—that we took for granted.

The decision we both faced rested on probabilities and a knowledge of disease transmission patterns. There had been no publicly reported outbreaks of viral hemorrhagic fever in Ethiopia, and cases of hemorrhagic fever cases tend to cluster because the virus particles are so infectious. And, for what it was worth, after lying in the clinic in Addis Ababa for several days, the Spaniard looked awful but was alive. It was scarce comfort, but most hemorrhagic viruses would have killed him by now.

Of course, there were certainly other infections that could be responsible for his illness: these included bacteria from a family known as rickettsia, which are transmitted by ticks; and others known as leptospires, which are found in fresh water. Viruses such as Yellow Fever, Dengue Fever, and Rift Valley Fever, all of which are transmitted by mosquitos, were also options.

Given that there had been large outbreaks of relapsing fever in Ethiopia and Sudan over the course of the year, it seemed likely that the Spaniard had contracted that particular bacterial disease, which is caused by Borrelia—large, spiral-shaped bacteria transmitted by lice and ticks. Borrelia can sometimes be seen on the same blood smear as malaria; but to find them, there needs to be enough bacteria on the slide, and the blood samples need to be taken specifically when the patient is shaking with an episode of fever and chills. They're easy to miss. Moreover, if it were Borrelia, it was already being treated with the antibiotics the patient had received.

This game of poker could only be played in the context of what was happening healthwise elsewhere in Ethiopia, even considering the really limited public health infrastructure and reporting. But we needed to make a decision. We couldn't spend the day on a runway with a feverish, bleeding patient.

Kione and I looked at each other, and then, without a word, we began to transfer the patient to the airplane stretcher together. Kione plugged in an IV line, and we put on masks and gloves. Then we loaded the wilted Spaniard into the plane. We closed the door and turned on the air conditioning, and the pilots aimed for a distant runway in the middle of a city of five million strangers. If our calculations were wrong, if it was hemorrhagic fever, then those strangers, Kione, and I could all be dead. If we were right, the Spaniard would recover, and we would emerge unscathed.

Emergency medicine is about beginnings. It is only infrequently about endings. Over the course of a career, we emergency care doctors will meet thousands of patients, listen to their symptoms and concerns, and make a preliminary diagnosis. In the face of limited information, we prescribe treatments and set the trajectory for a patient's next health care engagement. Usually, we are right—or at least directionally right—and our stabilizing therapies are generic enough that they are regret-free and allow for further investigation to narrow and fine-tune the diagnosis.

Occasionally, we are wildly off the mark: what might look like a sprained rib, for example, may ultimately turn out to be a heart attack. Presentations can be subtle; the patient may convince himself incorrectly—and us, too—that the pain was the result of a tennis game or a skiing fall. No matter how empathic we are, this kind of biased information flow can result in distorted decision-making.

When you are misled, or you just decide wrong, news travels fast. We are quick to hear about our errors—colleagues will be breathless with *schadenfreude* when telling us about a "bounce back" to the emergency department on a subsequent shift; or we will receive a call or a text from our internist colleagues with a twist to a diagnosis we had made. In the Spaniard's case, should we have made an error and taken a patient suffering from a highly infectious hemorrhagic virus to the city, we would be inundated with breathless internists—quite literally.

Generally, most patients ricochet through the system and diagnoses are confirmed or changed as information evolves. Most often, we emergency care doctors at the front of the funnel never hear anything more. Emergency medicine is the story of unknown endings. We must have faith in our work.

I'll tell you now that, in the end, everyone survived.

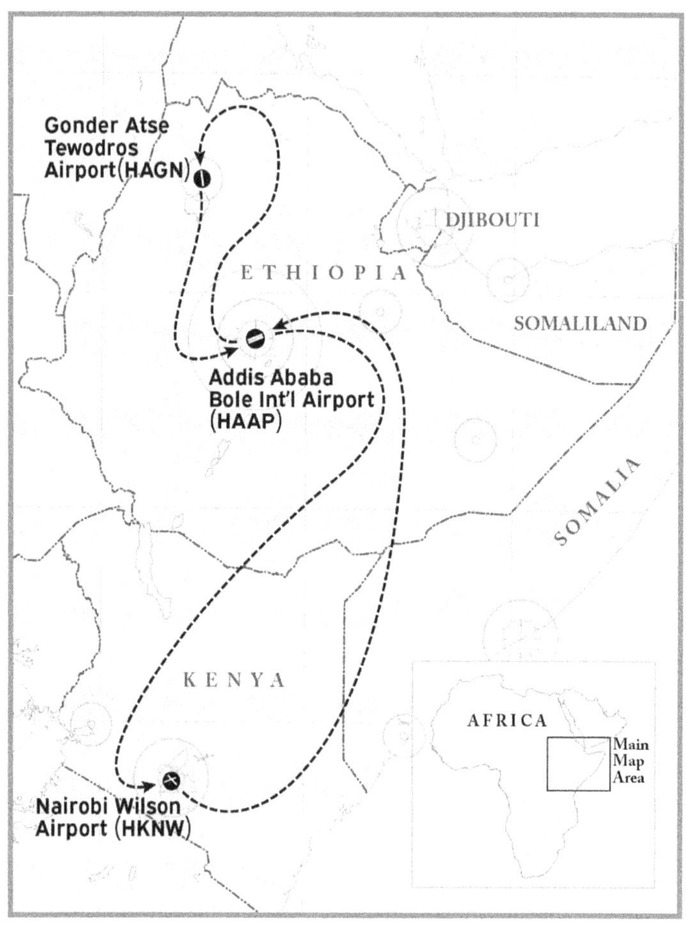

Evacuation from Gondar, Ethiopia, via Addis Ababa, using a Citation

NOMENKLATURA

The crowd doesn't have to know, all they have to do is believe and submit to being shaped.

— Benito Mussolini

I had been warned about Kafkaesque Ethiopian bureaucracy. A desperately sick Canadian teenager was waiting for us in Northern Ethiopia, and we were stuck on the tarmac in Addis Ababa dealing with the officials. The delays were infuriating. No matter how much we prodded and urged the Ethiopians to move more quickly, we were held hostage to the process, including stamps and seals and forms to be filed. We watched the captain haggling with a handling agent, several customs officers, one officious military representative wearing camouflage, and several young men in reflective vests who served no clear purpose.

This bureaucracy certainly wasn't unique to Ethiopia; in many capital cities, we had been forced to wait, or offer payments, or complete meaningless forms. But here, the bureaucracy and mindless process seemed to permeate every aspect of the trip. It was an odd experience, because next to our jet and the paperwork morass sat a sleek international terminal with well-maintained current jets from the modern Ethiopian flag carrier.

As I watched our process play out, I wondered if the airport represented a thin veneer of efficiency over a basically dysfunctional chassis. Outside of the modern airport, Ethiopia was one of the poorest and least developed countries in Africa. It was rated as a Least Developed Country by the United Nations on the basis of its per capita income—35 percent of its population lived in extreme poverty of less than $1.90 per day—its challenged health and literacy measures, and its economic instability. Paradoxically, and at the same time, Ethiopia had among the highest rates of GDP growth in Africa, driven by a pivot to manufacturing and recent foreign investment.

Poverty didn't necessarily explain why the bureaucracy was so much worse than other countries on the continent, or why there had been no attempt to expedite the process or waive requirements for an air ambulance that that they knew well.

We had left Nairobi bound for Gondar, Ethiopia, early in the morning on the Citation jet to retrieve a young Canadian man who was experiencing a serious diabetic emergency. Gondar is in northern Ethiopia, not far from Sudan and Eritrea. It's a historic, beautiful part of the country and is popular with adventurous tourists. But Gondar wasn't an official port of entry or exit, so before we could land at the small airport nearby, where our patient was waiting for us, we needed to stop in the Ethiopian capital, Addis Ababa. There, we needed to wait for officials and get their approval for fuel, inspections, military checks, and on and on. It would take us hours to navigate.

We eventually were allowed to leave Addis, and we began our second leg through Ethiopia. Once in the air, we crossed over the green fields and hills of Western Ethiopia and finally landed at the small airport outside the city of Gondar. Our arrival had been much delayed, and our young patient, who had been waiting in the back of a van on the tarmac for hours, had apparently taken a decided turn for the worse.

Diabetes is a tough disease. At home in Canada, our patient's life existed within narrow tolerances: a daily schedule, the same exercises and foods, and insulin delivered by a smart machine on his waist that kept his blood sugar in a certain tight range. But here, in northern Ethiopia, his physiology and his technology had been severely tested. The strenuous exertion of touring through Ethiopia, the new and unknown foods, the intense sun, and the traveler's diarrhea all had set him off balance, out of equilibrium. It wasn't that he had been carefree or careless, a footloose teenager on a trip away from home. He was not. His diligence was a habit of a lifetime of self-management—of thousands of shots taken in the morning, in the dark, sitting in his bedroom desk chair.

But in Africa, willpower and focus hadn't been sufficient. His blood sugar levels had begun to climb because of the physiologic stress his body was under. As such, he struggled to adjust his insulin doses to compensate. Without enough insulin (the key that unlocked sugar entry into the cell) to compensate, his body was unable to use sugar for fuel, and it turned to fat for energy, producing—as byproducts—ketones and acids that already had begun to accumulate. His own body's metabolism was poisoning him. His kidneys tried valiantly to compensate; he urinated and urinated until he was deeply dehydrated and nearly unconscious. His body, without his conscious thought, tried to remove acid in the blood by triggering deeper and quicker breaths, exhaling acetone and carbon dioxide. But these efforts were temporizing measures. Without correction of his dehydration and management of his sugar and insulin levels, he would die.

The pilots shut down the Citation's engines and opened the door so that we could exit. I quickly deplaned and hurried over to the van. When I climbed in the back doors, I could see that this young man was sick. Very sick.

Our patient was of college age, from a small town in Canada. He was alone; his friends had sent him to the airport from the hostel where he was staying. They had made sure he had his fanny pack with his passport, a few banknotes, and traveler's checks that came in ten-dollar denominations.

I knew the diagnosis immediately. The air in the van smelled sweet—a familiar, sharp, artificial floral smell. With every breath, he was exhaling volatile ketones. Looking at him, sunken-eyed and weak, I recalled photos of children's diabetes wards from the 1910s—rooms lined with rows of beds, filled with stick-thin little children breathing deeply, their breath also smelling of ketones until they died from their profound metabolic derangements. Medicine might have bought a little time back then, but diabetes was uniformly a death sentence for children. It was not until three smart Canadian surgeons injected newly discovered bovine insulin into those dying kids that doctors were able to watch the children resurrect in their beds, like miracles.

I could read the young man's face: he was relieved to see us, frightened but independent. His pride had been wounded. He seemed ashamed of the situation he was in. Brave enough to vacation in a remote area of Africa, he was now dependent on strangers.

We needed to move him to the aircraft, which was only fifteen feet away from the van; but, remarkably, the van's driver refused to move until he received permission from a security officer, no matter how sick our patient was. Until he received this permission, we were forbidden from getting out or walking across the painted line. The driver's behavior was inexplicable, even callous. I couldn't believe that anyone would adhere rigidly to meaningless regulations when someone's life was clearly on the line. Didn't he feel any urgency, any personal responsibility for his life? Thanks to the calcitrant officials in Addis and the ones here, our patient had become much sicker. But there was nothing we could do. Seething over the guard's lack of urgency, Michael and I sat silently in an old van, our patient panting and me tapping my foot, only meters from a veritable ICU, only separated by a painted line as we waited for the process to play out.

Someone eventually found a security officer. She was a fat and sour woman wearing a field coat and epaulets. She'd had to leave her lunch to come outside, and she now ambled over to the van, waved her hand dismissively, and went back to what she was doing. Permission granted. We hurriedly drove the short distance to the plane to begin our work.

In the plane, we quickly confirmed that we were dealing with severe diabetic ketoacidosis, or DKA. Our diagnostic process was straightforward: Michael started an IV and was able to collect a small sample of blood. We had two point-of-care lab test machines, and they confirmed that the young man's metabolism was wildly out of whack: his blood sugar was high—off the scale, really. Another test, using a portable blood gas monitor, confirmed that his blood was extremely acidic and that his electrolytes had been fiercely affected—including his potassium level, which would cause his heart to beat wildly if not managed. These findings, with the smell of ketones on his breath, confirmed the diagnosis of DKA.

Michael and I began the work of stabilizing the ill patient. We placed a second IV and began to rapidly infuse intravenous fluids to replace the liters of fluid he had lost.

Michael inserted a urinary catheter. Then, he mixed a small bag of insulin, and we set the IV pump to deliver a low, constant infusion of the lifesaving insulin our patient needed. The insulin would begin the process of correcting his metabolic abnormalities, but this correction would take days and need to be done slowly. Excessively fast correction, fixing in hours what had taken days to develop, could be lethal.

It was time to get going. But there was yet another delay. The captain stuck his head into the cabin and let us know that the airport superintendent was away, and we couldn't leave until he got back to give his staff the go-ahead. We may need to wait for a few hours till he was found. So, we sat again, effectively running a one-person ICU—though at least knowing this time that our patient, who was sleeping, was getting treatment.

From the cockpit, I could hear the captain arguing

over the radio with the tower, poking them every five minutes for an update, reiterating the urgency of our departure. They, too, were entirely unmoved by our predicament. The controller's voice was flat, unconcerned, and officious. Then, thirty minutes later, we somehow got the OK to take off. Despite the captain's best efforts, we would need to detour to Addis, once again, to clear yet more official channels on the way back to Nairobi.

By the time we landed back in Addis in the early afternoon, we were running low on the IV fluids we needed to keep infusing. Our patient was looking much better and had started making urine, but he remained profoundly dehydrated and was liters behind where he needed to be. We were regularly checking his blood gas measurements and making corrections to his fluid infusion—but, with the long delays on the ground, we simply hadn't brought enough IV fluid.

The plane had pulled onto a quiet area of the tarmac, and when the door opened, the captain was yet again running a bazaar with a mix of rubberneckers in camouflage and reflective yellow vests. I grabbed the captain's attention and asked if the ground agent, whoever he was among the tourists in vests, could request a few bags of IV fluid from the airport clinic, which we assumed sat just inside the shiny glass international terminal a few hundred feet away.

Predictably, this wouldn't be easy. As Michael watched with some amusement, I spoke with six officials of various stripes, including a soldier with an AK-47, an ambulance worker, and then the tower. I advocated for my patient: *He badly needed supplies which were widely available; we could pay cash for what we used; it would be an act of humanity. Was there someone in a senior role we could speak with? Could the airport doctor come and meet us?* One official sympathized and suggested that we take a taxi to a private hospital and then come back. He said it was five minutes away; another said it was thirty minutes away. Still another one said an hour, maybe, with traffic. The captain said that there was no way we'd be let back into the airport once I left; our immigration status, as crew, was vague.

Nobody at this international airport, which operated direct flights on state-of-the-art aircraft around the world, could seem to figure out how to get a few bags of IV fluid from a clinic. Nobody could make concessions for a dying man. I wondered if we hadn't played the game right. Maybe there was a trick to unlocking favors? Unlike in many other countries in Africa, in Ethiopia, it seemed that petty bribes—or, specifically, the absence of petty bribes—wasn't the issue. Nobody was hitting us up for money to make things work. The *process* itself was inviolate. I was truly gobsmacked.

It occurred to me, in a moment of reflection, that the bureaucracy we were dealing with was a remarkably Soviet experience. Indeed, Ethiopia was only fifteen years out from their twenty years as a Communist nation. These habits—the officiousness, the centralization of power, the unpleasantness, rigidity, and lack of willingness to make any concessions—were traits that the Ethiopians had learned from the Soviet Union and the Eastern Bloc. It was a legacy of the Soviet and American Cold War proxy battles in Africa in the 1970s. In Ethiopia, the Soviets had won, an event which would color Ethiopian culture for the next thirty-five years.

The Ethiopian Empire and culture go back almost a thousand years, to the 1200s. For seven hundred years, the country had successfully defended itself against invasions and maintained its independence. But in 1935, Italian Fascists, under Benito Mussolini, invaded and took over. After that, Ethiopian history would change. In 1941, the British threw out the Italians during World War II. Ethiopia went on to renew its independence in 1944.

Then, in 1974, a Soviet-backed military junta, called the Derg, deposed the eighty-two-year-old Ethiopian Emperor Haile Selassie, a descendent of the Queen of Sheba. He had been in power since 1930 (though he had been exiled during the Italian occupation). The Derg executed several former officials, assassinated Selassie in his bed in 1975, and turned Ethiopia into a Marxist-Leninist state. This all worked out poorly. Over the years, mismanagement by the junta and nationalization of both industry and land led to dramatic declines in agricultural productivity. Eventually, severe and well-publicized famines swept through Ethiopia. More than a million Ethiopians died.

Rebel forces finally overthrew the Soviet-backed People's Democratic Republic of Ethiopia, the Derg's successor, in 1991. By the late 1980s, the Communist Bloc (itself coming apart through Glasnost) had stopped financially supporting Ethiopia, which led to the weakening of the regime. It wasn't until 1994 that Ethiopia became a parliamentary republic.

Though the government had changed, and Ethiopia was a democracy, the sad legacy of communism seemed to be an emotional and cognitive scar on the country's ability to think nimbly and unconventionally. It was pure

Soviet. In that system of thought, centralization of power became the enemy of resilience. A top-down authority structure became the enemy of adaptability. Adherence to rules and standards made it ideologically opposed to irregularity, complexity, and the changing nature of life.

With nothing to show for our attempts to get IV fluid in Addis Ababa, Michael and I made the decision to push on once we got our papers, while trying to stretch our supply. The longer we waited, and the more we pinned out hopes on asking the system to flex, the worse the situation would become. So, the captain fired up the engines again, and after stashing a thick stack of papers in triplicate, with stamps and seals and signatures, he turned onto the Addis runway for the second time that day, and we accelerated toward Nairobi, which was a few hours away.

Despite the full day of wrestling with the bureaucrats, our patient was alive and looked far better than when we had arrived. In the air, every hour, Michael and I would draw a small blood sample to see how we were doing. We charted the data and made a line graph to ensure that we didn't overshoot our clinical targets. Doing so was a real risk. It would be much worse to move too quickly than too slowly. Establishing homeostasis is a slow, seductive dance; the young man's recovery would take days— probably a couple in the ICU, and then a few more in a floor bed where he would resume his home insulin and doctors would look for any signs of a predisposing infection, and where he could plan an early trip home to the Great White North.

I wondered how long it would take Ethiopia to reestablish its own homeostasis after communism—although perhaps life under the emperor, prior to 1974, was equally restrictive. Whatever the cause, the inflexible Ethiopian system demanded a top-down command structure which denied talented people at lower strata the ability to make smart, independent decisions.

In the West, we had learned over the years that more decentralized forms of management were nimbler and achieved better results than highly centralized ones. Giving an organizational goal and then reasonable freedom to front-line workers and managers to achieve that goal has been called one of the great characteristics of American management. A decentralized management style has also guided US military policy and allows for a fighting force, led on a daily basis by empowered junior officers and NCOs, to pivot quickly and make decisions on the fly.

Perhaps Ethiopia would get there, too, but I was skeptical. It was possible communism had created this extreme culture of bureaucracy in Ethiopia, but top-down management was a fixture in many countries throughout Africa and the Middle East. It flourished anywhere trust was low and overthrows were a concern. Over the subsequent years, I would find many other examples of top-down management in my work overseas. In those places, Americans were often hired to bring in a more open and employee-empowered model of management by senior leaders who recognized the competitive advantage it afforded. If they could achieve cultural change, it would be grindingly slow; average people had learned to keep their heads down.

Empowering people in positions of even modest authority to bend rules and try new things and take risks seemed to be the real secret for how to advance a country in the next millennia. But in Ethiopia, what had taken twenty years to build would take far longer to dismantle.

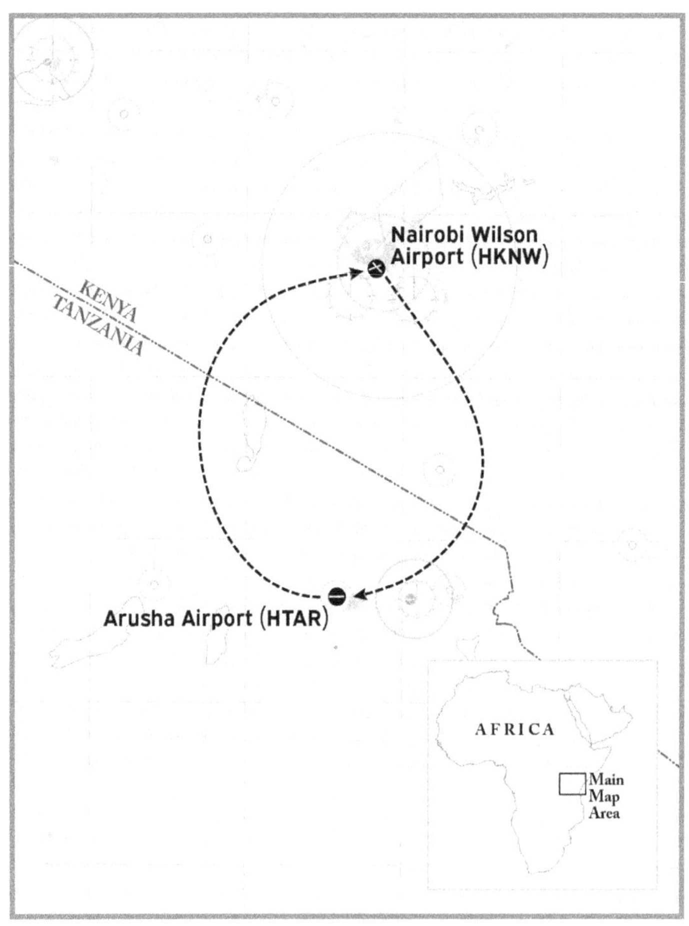

Evacuation from Arusha, Tanzania, using a King Air

WE ARE NOT GHOSTS

People think that epilepsy is divine simply because they don't have any idea what causes epilepsy. But I believe that someday we will understand what causes epilepsy, and at that moment, we will cease to believe that it's divine. And so it is with everything in the universe.

– Hippocrates

The villagers were chasing the European moviemaker's car when it flipped. Her driver, who came with the rental car, had become frightened by the crowd trailing behind the car—a group of angry men and women in T-shirts and sarongs and plastic flip-flops. They were running and screaming and waving their fists.

Only the filmmaker was hurt in the crash, and her injuries were minor. But she was shaken. She had good insurance and wanted to "get checked out" in Nairobi for a few days. She called the Flying Doctors emergency number directly. So, on that quiet and sunny weekend afternoon, we took off from Wilson Airport for a scenic flight, past Mount Kilimanjaro, to a remote runway on the Tanzanian border with Kenya.

We found our cinematographer inside a small wooden terminal, sitting on a bank of chairs, and looking altogether well. She seemed packed and ready to go, surrounded by several pieces of decent luggage that her assistant had carried from their replacement car. She was a handsome woman, young, self-confident, self-funded, and idealistic. She wore colorful billowing scarves, no makeup and no jewelry, and had her hair pulled back with a simple clip.

As we spoke, however, it was not the filmmaker who commanded my attention; instead, I carefully observed her assistant. He was a small man, quite short, and had been in the car when it rolled. He, too, seemed uninjured. He wore a Gilligan hat and dark glasses and had the same characteristically African facial features as the Tanzanians in the small terminal around him. But what interested me was that his skin was chalk-white, and he had tufts of tightly curled short white hair. He had albinism. I had never seen anyone like him before.

The pilots had gone to pee and begin the customs paperwork, and we had some time. It was cool and pleasant under the shade in the simple terminal; Tanzania was lush, the air fragrant. There wasn't much medically to be done for the filmmaker, other than a quick exam and vital signs. While we waited, she told us what had happened.

She was in Tanzania, she said, to document the plight of Africans with albinism. One in every 1,400 Tanzanians (compared with one in twenty thousand births in Western countries) is born with a gene that interrupts the production of melanin, leaving their skin and hair stark white. The albinism puts these individuals at risk for severe skin cancer and blindness. Most African people with albinism are dead by forty, usually of skin cancer.

But there was more, and a quick internet search confirmed the details. In Tanzania, there was a significant stigma attached to being born with albinism—so much so that sometimes albino children were left in the sun to "darken" by their parents, which clearly didn't help things. These unfortunate souls were always going to face a terrible life; they were treated as an underclass. They were shunned and unemployable, like lepers.

Worse, some Tanzanians believed that there was something magical and powerful about the flesh and hair of people with albinism. Native witch doctors had been known to prepare potions using the blood, bones, and skin of the exhumed corpses of albinos, because they believed the magic and power could be transferred. Albino hair was often woven by fishermen into nets for good luck.

This long-standing, latent superstition in Tanzania took a dark turn for the worse when a TV series imported from Nigeria became a popular phenomenon overnight. The soap opera's storyline dealt with a family tragedy and the good luck that albino body parts brought them. The series dramatically fueled the public's interest in witchcraft. Almost like an epidemic, a madness spread rapidly across the region. Albino talismans grew in value. Albino bodies and body parts began to fetch thousands of shillings in Tanzanian markets, and a criminal enterprise emerged to meet the demand for bodies. Packs of murderers, incentivized by massive payouts, began to prowl villages and kidnap and dismember albinos of all ages. Soon, few albinos left their houses.

It was hard to know how to respond to the allegations in the media, including the investigative stories coming out of Tanzania in reputable international newspapers. It seemed so farfetched—witch doctors and murderers-for-hire dismembering albino children in the night—that I was inclined to imagine that it was a trope, maybe a coarse reference to cannibalistic African tribes from years ago. But the reports of albino deaths and dismemberments were *legitimate,* and there were entire NGOs dedicated to protecting albinos. And it wasn't just in Tanzania; there was no doubt that there was a price on albino heads in other parts of Africa, too.

The documentary film crew had come to a small village in Tanzania to interview a family whose child had been murdered. They'd arrived without issue and, after setting up in the family's home, had begun filming interviews with the child's family and other villagers. But the questions and the parents' responses had made the villagers palpably uncomfortable. Someone angrily asked the cinematographer to stop filming and told her that her questions were inaccurate and from a different era. Then, at some point, someone got the local policeman.

Several villagers, by then, had worked themselves

into a rage. The family, on one hand, wanted their child's death publicized; the villagers, on the other, wanted to keep the story from international audiences. A small mob gathered outside the hut where the interviews were being filmed. At some point, someone started to yank the cameraman and the filmmaker out the front door of the structure. The producer, a cameraman, and two assistants grabbed their equipment and began to run for the car. Their driver had never seen anything like it. As soon as the car's doors were closed, he accelerated away from the hut and headed down a muddy dirt road at full speed.

The dirt road outside town in the Tanzanian savannah was bad in the best circumstances, but the group was in their utility vehicle, which had a high center of gravity and was loaded with equipment. A sudden drop-off of the shoulder of the road into a culvert caused a wheel to catch and the vehicle to flip dramatically on its side. The villagers, witnessing the crash, were apparently chastened by that point. Realizing they had gone too far, they simply turned around and walked away, shaking their heads.

At the airport, when the pilots returned, we walked over to the plane, loaded the filmmaker's luggage, and strapped in. Her albino assistant, now without the filmmaker's protection, was long gone—probably into hiding. I wondered suddenly how it would feel to be hunted for my body parts, looking over my shoulder, hearing noises in the night. The fear would occupy my day and color my every interaction with the world.

If I'm honest, my first response to hearing about the magic talisman was an eye roll. In health care, you'll find magic treatments everywhere—those homeopathies and potions and healing crystals of the clinical world. Magazines and television infomercials are filled with advertisements for supplements and creams that promise, without any evidence (and with disclaimers in small letters) better skin, better erections, and improved energy. The actress Gwyneth Paltrow has established an entire brand offering wellness and detoxification with a promise of enlightenment and empowerment. The Chinese have killed menageries of animals to create remedies of dubious value.

But we doctors tend to be judgmental like that, convinced that we offer real, science-backed therapies—or at least therapies that are *more* science-backed than those of other supposed healers. We have been pooh-poohing pseudoscience for years. In 1844, British physician

Thomas J. Pettigrew wrote in his book *On Superstitions Connected with the History and Practice of Medicine and Surgery:* "Man is a dupable animal. Quacks in medicine, quacks in religion, and quacks in politics know this, and act upon that knowledge. There is scarcely anyone who may not, like a trout, be taken by tickling … there is scarcely a disease for which a charm has not been given."

Ultimately, other than the destruction of irreplaceable wildlife, most of these supplements, potions, elixirs, crystals, and other woo-woo therapies are harmless, even if they aren't effective. For a so-called trout that has been tickled, the placebo effect of healing herbs may alone be worth the price of purchase.

But of course the situation in Tanzania wasn't about pseudoscience, and what was being offered wasn't a placebo. The hunting of people with albinism in Tanzania was a serious human rights crisis in a democratic country that had the rule of law and a bill of rights. Modern ideas co-existed with primitive beliefs. Sixty percent of Tanzanians, the majority of whom were Christian or Muslim, believed in the protective power of sacrifices to the spirits. It was the highest percentage in all of Africa. The murders weren't one-off attacks. And discrimination against people with albinism had become accepted practice for a decent subsection of Tanzanian society. The Tanzanian government, to its credit, had tried to catch and punish perpetrators.

Many Tanzanians felt deep shame when these murders were publicized. It explained the violent response that the filmmaker had received when the subject of her questions became clear. I understood the deep ambivalence of the villagers, their shame at this primitive practice being exposed to the world. East Africans wanted to be seen as progressive; talk of primal witchcraft-driven murders was a humiliation.

Sometimes, observing the region's uneasy vacillations was a reminder that East Africa was a complex cultural pastiche—a mix of tribal beliefs, animism, traditional witchcraft, and imported religions, all mixed with the demands of living in a global world.

It had been a trip to a faraway time, a profoundly odd call.

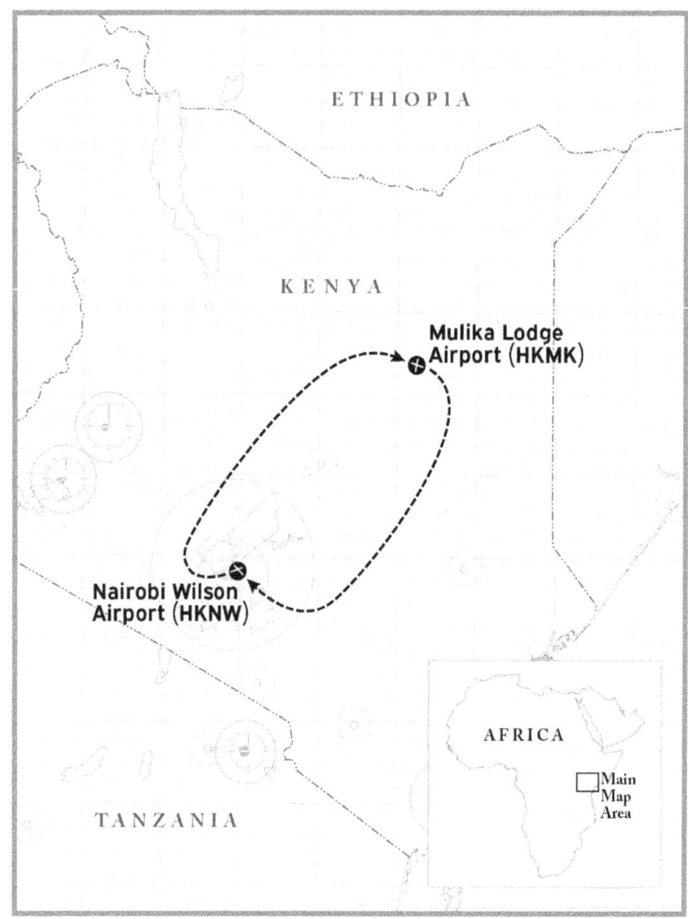

Evacuation from Mulika Lodge, Kenya, using a King Air

TICK TOCK

A Clock stopped –
Not the Mantel's –
Geneva's farthest skill
Can't put the puppet bowing –
That just now dangled still …

— Emily Dickinson

The EKG paper was the same brand that we used at home: an almost waxy, coated paper, white, with tiny red squares marking time and height, and easily smudged to black with a wet finger. This single page could show twelve different views of the heart's electrical activity, in three dimensions, as if the heart had been sliced with a sharp blade along twelve planes.

An EKG is an old technology; it is remarkably basic and has been in use since 1887. Representing voltage on one axis and time on the other, the squiggle of the EKG records the heart's electrical activity and how the heart is beating— whether too fast or too slow—and indicates whether its electrical "wiring" is connected and intact. It shows how electricity flows from the top of the heart to the bottom and how, along the way, it stimulates the heart muscle to contract and squeeze. The squeeze is usually a predictable ripple starting at the top of the heart and moving, with anticipated pauses, to the pointed muscular bottom of the heart. When there is damage to the heart, such as during a heart attack (a myocardial infarction) in which the small arteries feeding the heart become obstructed, the squiggles look different; experienced readers can tell which part of the heart is damaged from the pattern on the paper.

Even in the computing era, interpreting the twelve EKG tracings is a human endeavor—an art, really. There are separate and different lines moving up and down. Pulling together an interpretation is nuanced. It requires the doctor to think in three dimensions, and most doctors are bad at it. Cardiologists spend a lot of time arguing about interpretations amongst themselves; they seem to like the controversy. But studies show that they still make mistakes in about a quarter of their reads. Non-cardiologists are worse. Manufacturers put computers into the EKG machines, and those interpretations were often wrong, as well. In one study of computer-generated reads, the data showed that more than half of the automated readings had major errors, worse than those made by humans.

But here, sitting aboard the plane in Meru, Kenya, which itself was sitting on the runway, I felt confident that my read was correct. I'm not an unusually competent reader, but there was little risk of misinterpreting this EKG. It was awful. It showed a large myocardial infarction from a major blockage of an important coronary artery. The tracings, from multiple angles, were wildly elevated and sloped, indicating dead heart muscle. In those areas, the heart had been starved for blood and oxygen by a blockage in the artery that fed it. The blockage took out a watershed of tissue, including the main electrical pathway of the heart, which ran from the top of the organ to the bottom.

Myocardial infarctions are time-sensitive illnesses; they tend to devolve in a certain way over a period of hours and days. The ultimate outcome of the heart attack depends on where there is a blockage, how much muscle is affected, and how the heart's function is affected. The clock we use to measure the progress of the heart attack is the EKG, which records the condition of the heart over time. We use EKGs to follow the progress of a heart attack, ordering them sequentially to determine where a patient is in his illness and how quickly the damage is occurring. A patient's EKGs will evolve over time.

I knew, looking at the most recent tracing of the man in front of me, that his heart attack was in late stage. It showed that a lot of his heart muscle had been damaged; his electrical pathways were compromised. The top of his heart had fallen back on one slow intrinsic rhythm, while the bottom of the heart—the ventricles—had reverted to its own backup, intrinsic rate. The disconnection was almost complete; the independent flailing rhythms were like two caught fish thrown onto shore and gasping separately for oxygen. This third-degree block meant that the normal pacemaker of the heart no longer set the heart rate. The owner of this heart was totally dependent on whatever blood his languid ventricles could squeeze out. As I watched the tape, I could see they were managing only weak, slow beats. The pattern was dramatically worse than the EKGs the hospital had sent from the day before.

We were late in arriving to this emergency. Our patient had suffered his heart attack the previous afternoon. Wilson had received a call the evening before, but by then it was too late to launch a flight, and, overnight, things had gotten much worse for the patient. We needed to get to Meru, a city of about forty thousand people on the slopes of Mount Kenya. The closest airfield was the Mulika Lodge Airport, a small location with one asphalt strip and no lighting. The pilots told me that if we had received the call an hour earlier the evening before, things would have been different—it was a short flight, and we could have gotten in and out with light to spare. But the call came when it did, and by then the sun was setting and it was too dangerous to go. The coordinators decided, instead, to arrange for an evacuation at dawn the next morning.

Medical students learn that time is muscle, meaning that the extent of heart damage is directly correlated to how long it goes without blood flow. The definitive treatment for these sorts of heart attacks is opening the occlusion in the coronary arteries with either clot-busting medication or angioplasty, where cardiologists insert a catheter into the occluded vessel and restore its patency. Wait too long, and the damage is irreversibly done: the patient will either die or survive with heart failure—which, in some cases, is bad enough that the patient becomes a cardiac invalid for life. That night without definitive treatment meant that our patient's outcome was going to be much worse than it might have been.

At 7 a.m., we landed on the asphalt strip and taxied to a stop. Meru is spectacular. It's fertile and prosperous, the breadbasket of Kenya. We flew over lime-green fields overflowing with tea and grains, and somehow the place seemed better put together, more alive and prosperous and hopeful, than most places we had visited.

On the airstrip, the air was humid and dense and fragrant. Kione and I sat on the steps of the plane and drank coffee from Styrofoam cups in silence. Calls of the birds and insects filled the area. The vibrancy before us would stand in stark contrast to what we would see next.

After half an hour, a dust plume rose in the distance. We stood up and stretched as the plume grew closer. In a few minutes, we were ready, just in time for a standard African rattletrap ambulance to pull close and stop. We unlatched the rear door, which lifted upward, pushed by hissing hydraulic pistons. Inside, a mortuary-gray but elegant local man lay on a bare mattress, with his family crowded together on the bench seat. An anxious ambulance attendant, looking fidgety, sat opposite the family.

As one, Kione and I moved into the ambulance. Kione sat on the bench seat and connected our monitor to the patient. I knelt at his side. After the machine cycled a few times, we stared at numbers. They were far worse than the patient appeared. His pulse was extraordinarily slow, and his blood pressure was barely detectable.

We were told that the care at the local hospital in Meru had been pretty solid and the doctors there had done what they could. They had started several medications to support blood pressure and heart rate and to bridge the wait. But, somehow, before the patient left the hospital, the IV lines had been pulled for the transport to the field. For someone who depended on the medicines, the results were predictable. It had been a foolish decision. I ran through a number of possible scenarios in which such a decision could have been made: Maybe nobody wanted the precious IV pumps, which measured the medicines on a drip-by-drip basis, to leave the hospital? Or maybe nobody wanted to travel to the field? Or maybe the ambulance attendant wasn't qualified to handle certain medications, and nobody else was available? In any case, the decision had been a bad one, and we could easily have traveled to the hospital with our equipment rather than sit planeside with coffee, as nice as it was.

We got our patient onto our stretcher, and the pilots helped us lift the stretcher up through the rear doors of the plane. Kione plugged a new IV line into the patient's IV catheter and checked his blood pressure by hand. Checking his blood pressure like that is a formality we perform in hopes that the machine has led us astray—that the miserable numbers are an imprecision or machine error. But hand pressures are really a totem to reassure ourselves. They never yield any better answers than the machine; they simply buy us time to get our thoughts together. Kione reported back a blood pressure of 72/40 and a heart rate of 40.

By all rights, according to the vital signs, our patient shouldn't be conscious— but he was. Whether he would survive the trip was another question altogether. Like I said: bad, very bad. The slow pulse caused by the destruction of tissue from the heart attack wasn't allowing the heart to pump enough blood to keep the patient's organs perfused. We needed to get the heart rate and blood pressure up, while being thoughtful about not asking his oxygen-starved heart to work too hard. The definitive treatment was hours away; our task was to try to keep everything pumping and perfusing and to allow as little to break down in his body as possible. Ensuring that was my job.

We had some hard clinical decisions to make. I wanted to get the heart rate up, and there were a few options, the least invasive being medications. The most invasive was external pacing, where we would apply electricity to the patient's heart via pads stuck to his chest and basically run his heart via remote control. Each shock would trigger his heart to pump a beat.

Pacing hurts—imagine your chest being shocked sixty times a minute—and so it creates a lot of medical complexity; at a minimum, he'd need pain medication. At some point, it would be necessary to sedate and ventilate him to allow the shocks to continue all the way to Nairobi. But each of those sedative drugs has side effects; some even cause low blood pressure themselves.

The key here was that our patient looked far better than his numbers suggested he should. There is an old adage in medicine that says the doctor should treat the patient and not the machine. So, that's what we did: we started with the basics. I took a vial of a drug called atropine and slowly injected it into the IV line. I knew that atropine would have no effect; it works, rarely, to increase heart rate. But it doesn't have a lot of downsides, so it's always where to begin. As the medicine was going in (and, as expected, doing nothing), Kione was getting the infusion pump ready. He pulled a second liquid medication into a large syringe and, in his meticulous handwriting, labeled the syringe, put it into an IV pump machine, and primed it to be plugged into our patient's main IV line. Then we started a second drug called dopamine. It was a drug that would make the heart squeeze harder and faster, which would cause the blood pressure to rise. It comes in tiny doses that need to be titrated via a drip to a goal. I hoped that it would improve the patient's blood pressure, just enough.

Kione started the pump, and we watched. In only a few minutes, the patient turned from ashen gray to a more normal color and became more talkative, even smiling every so often. We cycled the monitor: the heart rate and blood pressure were better. That was as good as we were going to get—unless we became much more aggressive, which would likely not make things better at all.

Serious emergencies require you to balance care decisions: you have to be clear-eyed and honest. You can't minimize the seriousness of a case by pretending that the patient is better than he looks and that the numbers are wrong. Nor can you be afraid to act, to make a decision in the face of imperfect information. I've seen junior doctors, typically thoughtful and well-meaning internists, delude themselves in this way.

But you also don't want to over-treat. More care is in no way better than enough care. As I matured as a doctor, I came to appreciate the feeling of being smoother and more deliberate, a bit slower in my impressions and actions, and more clearheaded and confident. Experience had molded Kione and me into wiser clinicians. After several minutes, we were where we needed to be. Our patient looked less terrible, and we were in a better position to get him to Nairobi alive. I breathed a sigh of relief as I listened to the turn of the engines.

This was a survivable heart attack—but, as with all heart attacks, success depended on time. The longer our patient went without definitive treatment, the worse he would end up. At Flying Doctors, we had done the best we could to speed the transfer; we were there as quickly as possible, with the right stabilizing treatments on board. But we were one part of a larger whole. For faster care, our patients would need more and closer runways, lights at night, better roads that could allow for a road transfer to Nairobi, critical care transport staff, and so on. Our intensive medicine was only a stopgap.

These sorts of delays caused by lack of access to infrastructure would only become more common in Africa. When countries progress economically, the types of medical issues they witness change. The poorest countries spend their time dealing with malaria and HIV, hunger, and parasites. These are all serious problems, but they aren't necessarily time-sensitive. Patients can often wait at least a few hours or days to get care, and that care can be delivered in a clinic or even in the field—the type of care that Flying Doctors' Dr Anne Spoerry practiced during her forty years of treatments given at a card table under a tree.

But, as countries develop economically, their populations begin to experience what are called diseases of affluence: people's diets become richer, they become obese, and diabetes and heart disease become common. Trauma, mostly from car accidents, becomes a more regular occurrence. Kenya, like many of the more developed, middle-income countries in Africa, was experiencing an emerging epidemic of diseases of affluence: trauma, strokes, heart attacks, and the like. These were time-sensitive illnesses.

This emerging and different trend of illnesses created new pressures on the Kenyan health care system. For patients to survive, they needed urgent medical responses and complex in-hospital interventions: surgery in the case of trauma, and angioplasty or clot-busters and an ICU for heart attacks and strokes.

These situations were probably good for business. They made Flying Doctors more necessary than ever. But, like our patient was showing us, we could triple the size of the organization and have little meaningful effect on outcomes. A more rapid response to these types of emergencies would require infrastructure well beyond the scope of Flying Doctors. The planes and crew weren't the limiting factor. Harder things were: roads, bridges, runways and lights, transfer ambulances, and transport crew.

Aeromedical evacuation was never meant to be definitive care; it's not a fix for all that ails you. Medevac's role is to stabilize messy situations, to keep patients from getting worse, and to get them to where they can receive a cure (if there is one).

Kenya would likely see limited improvement in outcomes of time-sensitive illnesses until its overall development caught up. You can't improve medicine, anywhere, in isolation. Human wellness, as a holistic concept, depends on many things coming together simultaneously to turn the tide: food, public health, investment in hard infrastructure, housing, health care, law, and so on.

In that plane, in Meru, the EKG was a cardiac clock that ticked the hours from affliction to death. And according to the EKG I was reading, we were late, very late. It was time to bug out. Time was passing.

If we were fast enough, our haste might save a few extra millimeters of heart muscle.

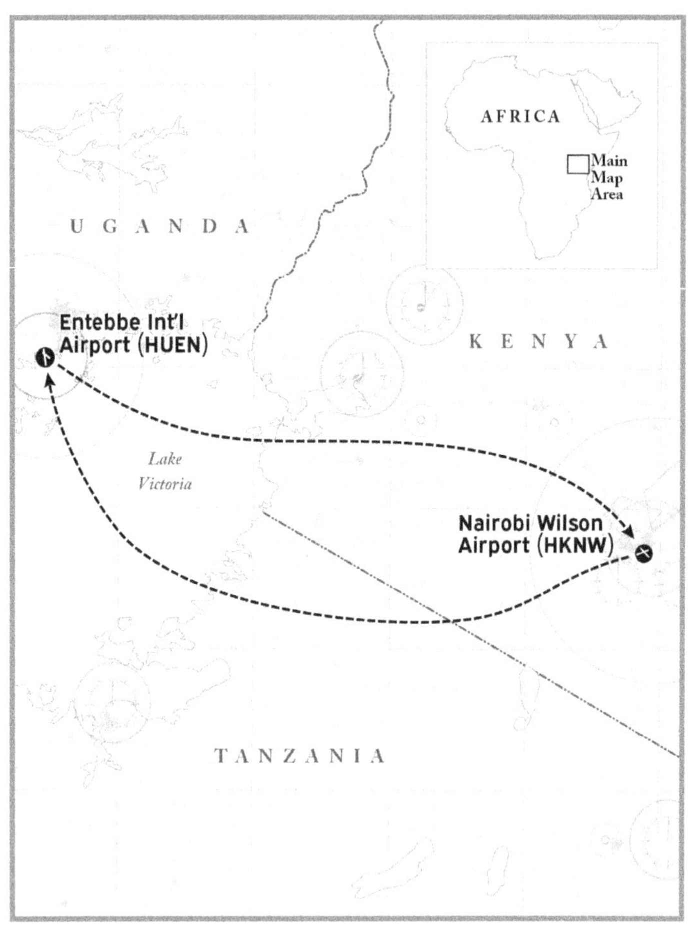

Evacuation from Entebbe, Uganda, using a Citation

INVISIBLE NETS

I went through life big-bang-bada-boom-bada-boom.

— Evel Knievel

It was thrilling freedom: being out in the world, a new graduate's first global internship, riding a motorbike through the markets of Kampala on a hot night. I've felt it. I've felt how different and vibrant and alive the city is in the evening. The humid air cools slightly but is still heavy and thick. The smells are amplified, intense, and powerful. The air is redolent of smoke from roadside grills and diesel fumes and garbage in the heat and fish and sweat. At night, the city is better-humored and more relaxed.

Kampala, a city that came together piecemeal over the years using an old British fort as a nidus, remains among Africa's fastest growing cities. Over the years, there had been several attempts to create a master city plan, but none of them took, and Kampala grew organically and slightly haphazardly. It was a pretty, green town whose streets had few right angles. In the center of the city, off the main highways, smaller backstreets were filled with markets. Against corrugated tin walls that obscured empty lots where buildings were razed, though not rebuilt, vendors set up tables of trinkets and warm soft drinks for sale. Matatus and bikes and pedestrians fought for space along busy roads with no sidewalks. There were hundreds of shops, selling tea and traditional food, poultry, air tickets, tours, and tooth extractions. Traffic moved iteratively, drivers seizing one sliver of opportunity at a time, keeping a sharp eye on the other drivers looking for the same opportunity.

In the outdoor market, when the harsh fluorescent light flooded the street from first- floor shops, it was sometimes hard to tell if the road was paved or not; maybe it was just old asphalt covered in inches of compacted dust. Inside, the barbers hung pictures of all the variations they offered clients, from 1950s to punk.

There were cellphone cards, cheap menswear pieces, and pots and pans for sale. Every so often, there would be a modern illuminated sign, inevitably for a bank or gas station with a security guard seated on a cheap stool just outside.

It was disorienting. I can easily understand how the crash had happened. On that boisterous late Saturday night in the markets of Kampala, two Australians—a young couple in lust—were riding a rented motorbike together. An impact with a car at a high speed had badly crushed them both.

The driver of the car, maybe seeing what he had done and judging the complicated implications of hitting two white kids, had fled from the scene. A cracked motorcycle and two twenty-somethings, their bones sticking through their scraped and torn blue jeans, were left bleeding in the road.

Emergency doctors, the world over, all have stories of busy nights caused by full moons and jinxes and bad luck. When people and objects collide, we also call them "accidents," but we know, of course, that most injuries aren't supernatural or random events. Patients aren't always blameless. Sometimes they do it to themselves. There will always be a few unfortunate people who have flowerpots fall on their heads from balconies above. But there will be many more patients who have made bad decisions. There will be ninety-year-olds on ladders; sixteen-year-olds drinking wine coolers in rebuilt Camaros; six-inch heels on cobblestone streets; men who train alligators and pop wheelies on dirt bikes. We care for all of them. For them, it's about freedom, feeling alive, repressing fears of bad outcomes, and being in the moment. Motorcycle-riding in the dark in urban Africa was one of those things.

After the crash, someone somehow scraped the Australian kids off the road and put them in a pickup and dropped them at the Kampala hospital. The doctors took X-rays, washed and patched wounds, stabilized broken bones, and watched as the young woman's oxygen levels began to fall. This was unexpected. She then developed a tight chest pain deep inside her lungs, and her face became a lighter shade of pale. The fractures were bad, but there was something else going on. Something worse.

Midmorning, after the paperwork had been sorted and calls had been made between Kampala and the embassy and the insurance company and a frantic family in Sydney, John and I were dispatched from Wilson in Nairobi to the airfield at Entebbe, which was only a thirty-minute drive to Kampala. We were headed back to Uganda, back to Kampala's dark public hospital.

John and I cleared customs with our equipment and entered Uganda. Once outside, we walked past the taxi hawkers and met the ambulance in the passenger pickup area. I got into the front passenger seat, and we headed from the airport to the hospital in Kampala. Our driver insisted on driving with lights and siren to get us through the traffic, as if the extra ten minutes would make a difference, and he accelerated down dirt roads as UN SUVs and passenger buses and bicycles and mopeds dutifully pulled over to let us pass.

We were there for the young woman; she was the sicker of the two victims. A different crew would come for her boyfriend later. When we arrived at the hospital, we found our patient lying in a bed at the back of the emergency ward. She was young and athletic. Her hair was pulled back in a ponytail, and she wore no makeup. In the bed, she looked shrunken and chastened and frightened. She lay on a bare, black plastic mattress, her leg pulled up at a sharp angle toward the ceiling, held by a rope and pully system which looped around a bracket and ended at the floor, where it was weighed with rough iron blocks. She was breathing oxygen from a washed and reused plastic mask attached to a large tank of oxygen on a wheeled metal cart.

John and I had a few things to work through. Our patient had lost a lot of blood, and her leg would require careful handling and surgery, that was for sure. Aside from her obvious broken thigh, though, her visible injuries didn't seem severe—just bruises and cuts and large abrasions. These would heal. What *was* concerning was her worsening breathing and decreasing oxygen levels, both signs that there was a more significant problem.

One possibility was chest trauma. Maybe broken ribs? Or a collapsed lung? I inserted the stethoscope tips in my ears and listened to her chest: there was good airflow throughout the lungs, making a collapsed lung unlikely. There were no external signs of chest trauma, either. John pointed to a stack of X-rays next to the bed, and I grabbed the chest images, printed on translucent sheets of film. Holding them up to the light coming through a window, I could trace the edges of the lungs. Their edges were immediately adjacent to the inner pleura of the chest wall. There was no collapsed lung.

There was, however, an ominous option that couldn't be seen on film: blockages in her lung capillaries caused either by blood clots or bits of fatty marrow from her broken femur, called a fat embolus, that had travelled to her lung. Either of these conditions, if bad enough, could kill her. She would need a CT scan of her chest to attempt to distinguish the two conditions. This step was important, because the definitive treatment for a blood clot in the lungs, called a pulmonary embolism, is to administer anticoagulants, strong medicines that prevent blood from clotting and keep blood clots from expanding. Without this medicine, clots can grow dramatically and kill by squeezing off blood flow through the lungs. You can breathe as hard or fast as you want, but it won't help. It's a circulatory problem, and it's a nasty way to die.

However, when you have a situation with trauma, particularly with something as severe as a broken thigh, the challenge is that blood thinners, which will treat a pulmonary embolism, will also cause already traumatic bleeding to worsen, sometimes severely. The hospital in Nairobi would need to distinguish between a fat and blood embolus. Until then, we would buy time with oxygen.

Palliating a broken femur is primitive, but effective: our goal is to straighten the femur, keeping sharp bone shards from spearing adjacent muscle. Until surgery can be done, we straighten the bones using a device a bit like a medieval rack. Thigh muscles are the strongest in the body, so doing this right requires mechanical advantage. We grab the ankle and pull, hard, and then attach a strap to the foot and attach the other end to a winch and begin cranking. This creates a decent amount of force and, done right, pulls the bone fragments apart. The patient fights, initially. Voluntarily or not, the thigh muscles contract against the force of the crank—but, with perseverance, the thigh muscles finally release in exhaustion. The patient's leg suddenly lengthens, and bones straighten. I've heard that pulling the bone into alignment and getting the sharp shards out from the adjacent muscle is a relief, but it looks brutal. The trick is to keep the tension on the line, without releasing it at all; if left unopposed, the muscles will reinsert the bone shards back into the tissue. It's a particularly tricky scenario when done on a moving stretcher, which we were going to have to do.

Getting to the plane was a miserable experience for all of us. To prepare, in the ED, we shifted bandages and splints and the hospital's traction devices, substituting larger weights for our smaller and more mobile pully traction splint. It would have to be secure; we would keep the traction steady to get the unstable fractures across miles of poor roads and a long flight. John injected a slug of morphine into the young patient's line, and the group of us moved her bit by bit to our stretcher, and then out the door of the hospital.

Our patient was lucky to be alive. Trauma in the developing world is common and predictable: roads are terrible, laws are not enforced, seatbelt use is lax, and drivers couldn't care less. Kids everywhere will be foolish, but I wondered if the two of them had any idea of the risks they had taken. These were young Australians who had grown up perhaps unaware of the complex system of public health and safety that was hardwired into their daily lives at home, and invisible to the point of not being noticed by them.

Actually, most of us pay little attention to the public safety net as we go about our daily lives in the West. Public health and safety are ever-present benefits of our daily lives: our food is automatically monitored for pathogens, our building and fire codes protect us from fire risks, and our medicines are checked for quality. When we drive, we travel on roads which must meet certain design standards for safety; we have and enforce traffic laws, helmet regulations, and speed limits. We license drivers, forcing them to display competence before taking the wheel. If the worst happens, we have modern trauma systems. This means that we never fully understand the risk profile of doing risky things, of chasing "freedom," because the downsides of doing those risky things have already been heavily mitigated. You can choose to ride a motorcycle fast in Australia, and if you crash there, the collision avoidance systems on other driver's cars, your mandatory helmet, your mandated cycle training, and the ready availability of paramedics will seriously limit your downside. It's surprisingly hard to truly be a libertarian in the West. A certain population of people work hard to pull it off—but they really should try it in rural Africa.

Africa, of course, has few of those Western protections. It leads the world in the rate of road traffic deaths per population, with a proportion more than twice that of Europe. Low-income countries have 1 percent of the world's vehicles but suffer 13 percent of the world's road traffic deaths. In high-income countries, 40 percent of the world's vehicles contribute to only 7 percent of the world's road deaths. The proportion of road traffic deaths per hundred thousand people decreases inversely to income; the lower the income, the higher the proportion of deaths. In Africa, there is a 20 percent difference in deaths between its middle-income countries and its low-income ones.

I wondered if understanding the extent of these risks would have caused the young Australians to reconsider their activities. Given that bungie jumping was a popular activity for young foreign tourists on the Nile, only thirty miles from Kampala, I doubted it. There, jumpers leapt forty-four meters off a tower, touching the river with their foreheads, before the elastic bands on their feet yanked them back. A tour-booking site noted that the activity was quite safe, since the cords were made of "high-quality white latex rubber, which is used by the best underwear manufacturers worldwide." Quite an endorsement.

John and I rolled our young Aussie patient through the ED and out toward the ambulance bay, passing her boyfriend on our way. He hadn't been hurt as badly, and another Flying Doctors crew had already been dispatched to collect him. He looked like a dope any parent would want their daughter to avoid. I imagined that he would feel stupid about having been so cavalier in such a high-stakes environment—but who can decipher the brains of late adolescents?

Back in the ambulance, the driver managed to navigate the undulating streets of Kampala as he drove toward Entebbe, while we maintained traction on the girl's thigh. We all made it through the gates of the airport in one piece. It later dawned on me, halfway through the trip, that our own odds of crashing in our speeding ambulance driving fast with lights and siren in Uganda had not been low. When we finally—and safely—arrived at the Entebbe airfield, we loaded the plane, secured the leg as best we could, and then set out for the quick flight across the border. We'd be at the hospital shortly, and there would be scans and surgery. The girl's leg would need to be fixed; but first, the doctors would need to determine if there was indeed a pulmonary embolus.

Economic development in East Africa had, on one hand, contributed to the increase in diseases of affluence I had witnessed. But on the other hand, it had allowed middle-income countries to spend funds on improving roads and introducing public safety campaigns. In any case, there was no doubt that you had to be careful in Africa. The risks to life were dramatically higher than at home. The invisible public health safety net, if present at all, was thinly woven, and perhaps not made of the finest white latex rubber.

As we came in for the landing at Wilson, our patient was in a deep, opiate-hazed sleep. I flipped through her chart from Kampala. On the last page of the chart, a nurse had written a note, in proper British grammar school script:

> *Flying Doctors: when you arrive in Nairobi, please call the patient's mother, Susan, in Sydney, to inform her that you have arrived without incident. Please be aware that she is quite cross about her daughter's remarkably poor decisions and will bring her home as soon as practical. She is mad with worry.*
>
> *Sincerely, Martha,*
>
> *Registered Nurse*

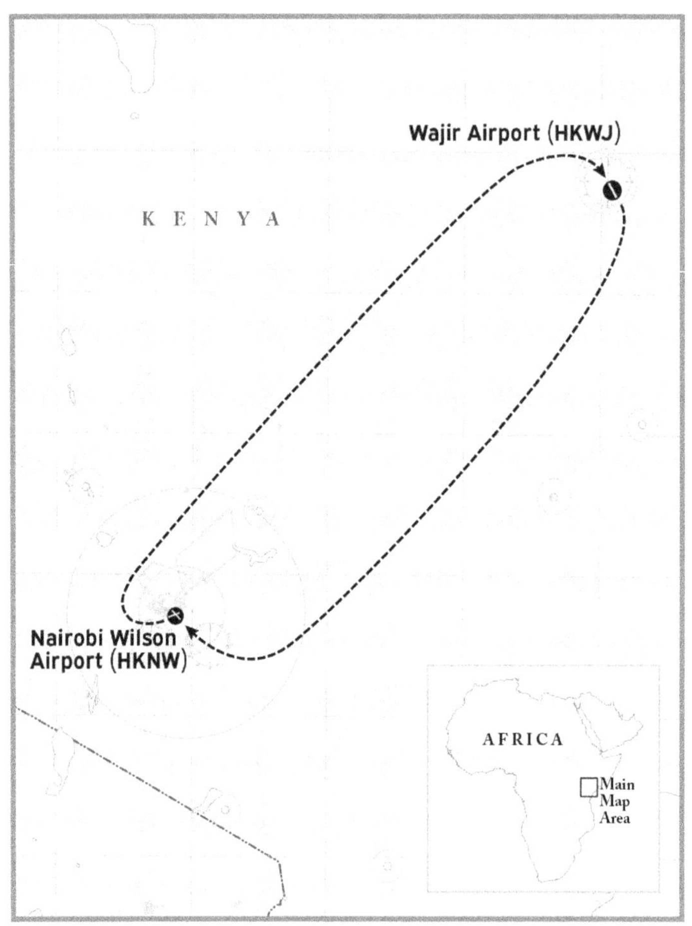

Evacuation from Wajir, Kenya, using a King Air

ALIENS

We are not human beings having a spiritual experience.
We are spiritual beings having a human experience.

— Pierre Teilhard de Chardin

At four in the morning, on my way to the hangar and halfway through the airport grounds, I found myself, surprisingly, in the middle of a khat bazaar. If I hadn't been up early, I'd have never seen the massive halogen lights outside the Wilson hangars illuminating large bundles of bush trimmings that groups of Somali men had carried out of the cargo doors of several twin-engine turboprops.

Arabs and Somalis are fond of a leaf from a shrub called khat. They chew these leaves, which act as a stimulant. It's not cocaine, by any means—but while legal in Kenya, it's restricted in many countries. Even in places where it's tolerated, the use of khat feels slightly illicit. There was a big market for it across all of East Africa, but mostly in Somalia. Wilson appeared to be the region's major trading hub.

Khat leaves are perishable and need to be fresh; as such, the perimeter of Wilson thrummed with an urgency not unlike that of the Tsukiji Tokyo fish market in the mornings. Planes carrying bundles of the crop flew in from fertile parts of Kenya, mostly from the Meru area, and porters carried the bundles to the long tables and tarps which had been laid out in one of Wilson's parking lots. For two hours every morning, except on Fridays, traders haggled loudly in Arabic and Somali and Swahili. Deals were done, and porters would carry the bundled khat leaves out to pickups or load them into the backs of planes for regional distribution. Most of the khat was sent to Somalia and the Arab world; some went overseas to the Somali diaspora.

The farmer's market was ephemeral. It turned into a pumpkin when the clocked ticked 6 a.m. By the time the secretaries and hangar workers arrived to work, the earthen lot would be swept clean. Nothing would remain of the vibrant market and the thousands of shillings that had traded hands only minutes earlier...except for a few leaves in the dust.

That morning, I sat in the dark in the back seat of a taxi watching a world forbidden to me. There was something unexpected and captivating about the market. It was a place where I didn't belong, where my presence could be seen as a trespass, where I was as an outsider. An unwelcome outsider. I had no idea how the bartering worked or how to read the hand signals that the traders shared. But I knew that I was watching something alien, not at all of my world. This parking lot I walked through every morning on my way to the hangar suddenly felt unrecognizable.

I wondered what might have happened if I'd left the safety of the taxi and entered the market. I had learned over the years that, no matter how foreign a situation seemed, if I could allow myself to be vulnerable, my courage would often be rewarded with a glimpse into a new world. Before that day in the khat market, I had experienced such a moment exactly twice.

Years earlier, I spent a weekend at Jebel Shams, a

mountain in rural Oman. I rented a car and planned a day hike up one of Oman's tallest peaks. It was hot, and the trails were arid and remote, really just paths worn into rock that had been eroded over the years. The cliffs of Jebel Shams formed into deep valleys which I descended, alone, as sunset approached. The call to prayer was suddenly issued from the minaret of a small mosque in the rural hamlet I had just passed. The urgent cry rose and echoed across the valleys in an otherworldly way. I was exhausted from the hike but mesmerized by the sound. Almost unconsciously, I ascended the trail and let myself through the back door of the simple, poured-concrete mosque. I removed my shoes and sat on the carpeted floor at the back of the small room, hoping that I wouldn't attract attention. Three men, freshly washed and shoeless, walked in and lined themselves in a straight row. They prostrated themselves in prayer. I expected to be thrown out; but, somehow, I was permitted to sit quietly in the back and experience the intensity and reverence in that room. It was an unexpected moment, something well beyond what I knew. I was deeply, transcendentally moved by the experience.

Twenty years earlier, I had been in a similarly profound though very different place. I was an eighteen-year-old EMT student on a clinical rotation, working out of the teaching hospital for the first time. I was taking vital signs and asking patients about their medical histories when an unexpected door opened. A car had run into a pedestrian at full speed, and now she was on a stretcher being hurriedly pulled by medics toward the trauma room. The head nurse saw the medics rushing to the trauma bay. She glanced at my temporary student ID badge, grasped my arm, and pulled me through a curtain into the trauma bay to await the dying woman. She pushed me against the wall, where the other students stood. "Watch," she said.

I stared at the spectacle. The doctors and nurses quickly began their well-choreographed routines. First CPR, and then surgical lines and airways; scalpels bloodlessly cutting the woman's pale chest; and blood dripping from a bag, swirling with clear saline and disappearing into a vein. It was a gruesome effort, futile in the end, and something that few people would ever witness. Before the family would be allowed back, the nurses tidied the sheets and hid the IV lines and had the floor mopped. When the tearful husband entered the room, there was nothing to betray the frenetic efforts that had been underway only moments earlier. It was as though a crack into another world had been sealed shut.

The khat market may have been the third such moment. What these experiences all shared, I realized, was that they were glimpses into unusual places that would be hidden to me under usual circumstances. Each fleeting moment felt like a rift in space. Each left me feeling quite small and foreign. Each one reminded me that there was a world well beyond my own narrow frame of reference. Yet, these same glimpses also reassured me that I could somehow manage the unfamiliar—and possibly even learn something new.

I watched that khat market for several minutes, until the taxi driver became impatient and began to slowly drive away toward the AMREF hanger. Reluctantly, I turned away from the car window. In a certain circuitous coincidence, our flight would take us in the same direction as many of the khat freighters, who were returning to the North.

Our flight was quickly ready to go, but there was a short line of flights ahead of us, waiting to take off. Once we got clearance and the King Air lifted off, the pilots pointed the plane northeast. We were headed to Wajir, a heavily Islamic area of Kenya near the Somali border.

Jana, the nurse on duty that morning, briefed me: a little boy had been hit by a fast car outside his hut days earlier. The family were pastoralists who lived far from town, and they had hired a taxi to bring their boy to the regional hospital. When they arrived, they learned that the only surgeon in the county had just left for Nairobi to attend a conference. The little boy sat in the ward for the night, his abdomen filling with blood, while the nurses frantically called Nairobi and tried to coordinate a transfer. We were to be that transfer.

Onboard the plane, we watched as the sun rose and the land around Wajir became arid, rust-red in color, and empty but for the occasional nomadic hut. After flying for several hours, we gradually began to approach. The gear descended, and we touched down on the airport's sole runway and then taxied to a red-roofed terminal building.

We were the only plane on the tarmac. There were several military buildings in the distance. Across the field, I could see the heavily guarded airfield gate lift open. A Toyota Land Cruiser ambulance from the hospital pulled through the gate and stopped next to our plane. Jana and I climbed down the airstairs and through the truck's back doors. Inside, as promised, a six-year-old sat limply in his mother's lap and looked at us, expressionless. It had been almost two days since the boy had been hit by the car—it had taken a day for the family to get to the hospital, and another twelve hours to arrange for a transfer.

I sat on the bench seat and tried to smile reassuringly at the frightened parents. They briefly returned my smile and then both looked away, shyly. We had no way to communicate other than expressions and hand signals; neither Jana nor I spoke a word of Cushitic.

I moved next to the stretcher and sat on the wheel well, next to the boy and his mother. I began a quick survey of the boy's injuries as he eyed me warily. His vital signs were OK, and I saw no evidence of a head or spinal injury. His lungs were clear, and his breathing was easy. But the boy's bruised, shiny, and distended abdomen revealed an obvious problem. His tiny belly button was stretched taught, protruding through his dirty T shirt, as if he were in the third trimester. As I examined his abdomen gently, the boy winced but didn't cry out.

I had leaned over the mother to listen to the little boy's abdomen with my stethoscope. Wearing a dusty abaya and khimar head scarf, the mother watched silently as I examined the bruised and bloody child in her lap. I suddenly became conscious of the few inches that separated us and worried about making her feel uncomfortable. She didn't seem to care.

It would be a two-hour flight back to Nairobi and to the pediatric surgeon who would need to find and plug the source of bleeding in the boy's abdomen. In preparation for the flight, we gave the boy a small amount of maintenance IV fluid. Jana pushed a dose of morphine into the line. I watched the medication take effect: the boy's face loosened, and his eyes closed. He slept for the remainder of the flight.

In the plane, I looked carefully at the young parents, who seemed about as comfortable as fish on bicycles. Jana had showed them how to use the airstairs and fasten their seat belts. They had never flown before, and the father, who looked to be in his mid-twenties, sat cross-legged on the seat, nervously tapping his cheap plastic sandal. He clutched a plastic bag of stained and what looked to be hurriedly assembled papers. His wife seemed to be in her early twenties. She sat next to the stretcher and couldn't bring herself to look out the windows; throughout the flight, she looked at her son, as if maintaining a vigil, and held his hand as he slept.

I could only imagine how hard this situation was

for them to process, to try to understand. They looked stunned; they were bravely doing their best to save the life of their son. At my core, I understood the stark power imbalance: our plane, my uniform, our incompatible languages, our skin colors, my papers and their papers, their dying child, and my medicines. It was like nothing they'd ever seen or known.

We were all strangers—to each other, to Wajir, and to the environment in the plane. I was new to Africa, after all. The family's eyes moved around the cabin, stopping on the leather seats and the burled wood wainscotting, a legacy from the jet's days as a corporate convenience. They absorbed this temple of medicine and high technology, this hidden space where profound things happened. That day, we all felt like aliens in a strange land as we shared in each other's humanity.

As I cared for the boy, I was overcome by the remarkable poignancy of the moment, our sense of human connection despite our differences. This family and I could not have been less alike. We shared no mutual points of reference; we shared no language, customs, religion, or culture. Our diets differed, as did our educations and holidays, and our marriage, birth, and death rituals. Yet, for a few hours, a mother held her most precious little boy close and then opened her arms and offered him to me. She trusted that I, a stranger with a stethoscope, would help and not take from her what little she had. The moment weighed on me. I felt a profound sense of responsibility and gratitude that she had taken me into her confidence. It was the kind of trust that medical students hoped to engender in our patients—a kind of trust that we come to learn is rare and fleeting. Her gestures of that trust—climbing into the plane, allowing me to examine her wounded little boy—were deeply meant, and deeply felt in return.

The flight was uneventful, and the boy remained stable for its duration. I took pleasure in watching the family peek in amazement out the windows and at one another as we approached the Nairobi sprawl. After the pilots landed, we taxied to the AMREF tarmac and then transferred to the waiting ambulance.

These were unsophisticated, unspoiled people who, like most parents, were prepared to bravely suffer any danger—to ignore their fears—to save their child's life. I watched them, newly able to put on their seatbelts in the ambulance, and felt a paternal urge to protect these simple people from the city. Despite my relative newness, it was far more familiar to me than to them.

By lunchtime, we had dropped the boy and his parents at the pediatric section of the Kenyatta ED. I had no idea how they would get home at the other end of this, but that would be a problem for another day. As we packed up, the family looked at us from their cubicle in the ER, and the boy, who hadn't engaged much, shyly waved goodbye. During the entire experience, none of them ever spoke a word to Jana or me.

We had all been strangers, opening ourselves to protocols we didn't fully understand, trusting that those around us would treat us with openness, tolerance, and grace. We were spiritual people having a deeply human experience. Our lives had intersected the two most fundamental elements we did have in common: our humanity and our caring for that little boy.

It was a reminder to leave the safety of the taxi. Be courageous. You'll be welcomed into new places you could only imagine.

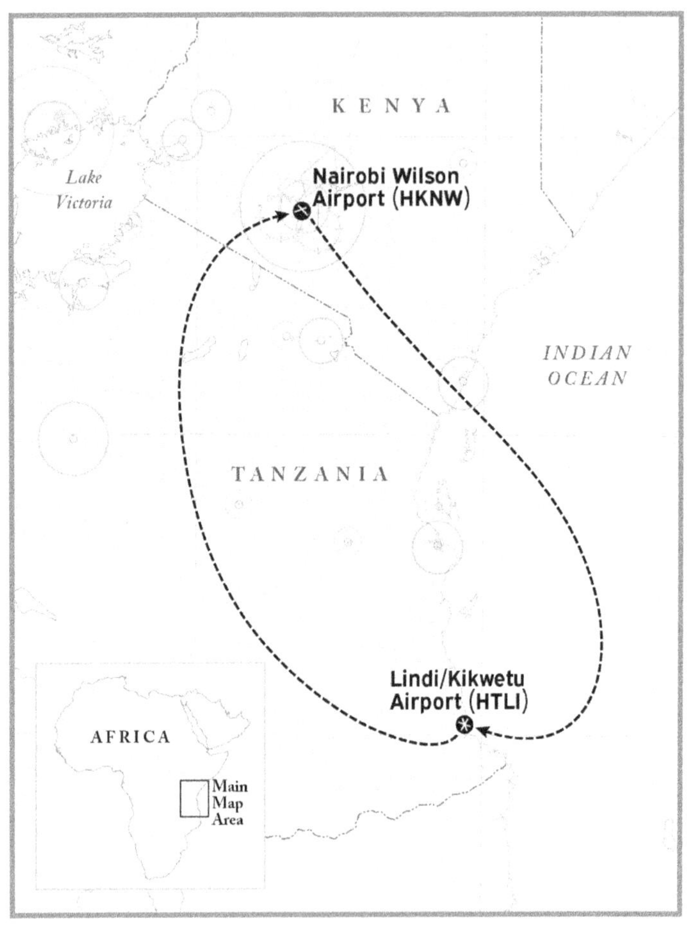

Evacuation from Lindi, Tanzania, using a King Air

MUDPILES

Sola dosis facit venenum … the dose makes the poison.

— Paracelsus

Our patient was small and shy and pale, just fifteen, with thick blonde hair, a small nose, and pretty features. She wore bedazzled jeans, a simple T-shirt, and a pair of fashionable sneakers that she'd brought from home on her last trip back. Her family had been in Tanzania for months, having moved from South Africa; her mother and father were both UN workers—idealists, maybe. In a moment of candor, while we were medevacking her daughter to Nairobi, the mother said that the family's transition—really, the girl's transition—to a new home had been rough.

The girl had been frightened when she saw the King Air arrive at the tarmac in Tanzania. Our very presence was confirmation that she was sick. As teens will do, she had acted rashly and seriously underestimated the effects of those actions. She now faced the reality, maybe for the first time in her life, that her own choices could put her in real danger. She had been impulsive, wanting to show the world how angry, hurt, and lost she felt as a stranger in a foreign land. It had been her bad luck that some of the pills in the cabinet were far deadlier than others.

She hadn't waited to tell her parents what she had done; she'd just carried the bottle from the bathroom and begun to cry. Her parents' hearts broke when they first understood, and then they panicked. Acting in unison, they rushed her to the car and packed her into the back seat for the long ride to the clinic. The girl laid down in the back. As her body metabolized the medicine, she began to feel unwell. They stopped the car long enough for her mother to move into the back seat and hold her daughter's head. The girl became dizzy and closed her eyes, and then she became sleepy. She laid against her mother and began to breathe deeply. Increasingly panicked, the father tried to drive fast. But the dirt road was terrible, and the father had to slow down for countless undulations and large holes. Their progress was a series of fits and starts. Picking up his cell phone, he dialed the clinic, telling them they were on the way and to expect them at the front door.

In the back of the car, the daughter became increasingly confused and agitated. Her mother tried to reassure her, to calm her. But the girl suddenly screamed loudly, only once, and then collapsed, falling sideways and striking her head on the window. She began to convulse, her whole body moving in spasms, her face frozen in a tight grimace of muscle contractions. Occasional wet exhalations burst from her pursed lips. The full-body seizures continued without stopping for the rest of their panicked ride to the clinic, another thirty minutes. The mother held her daughter and tried to keep her from choking on vomit and saliva. She tried to keep her daughter's head from hitting the door handles. When they pulled into the clinic, at high speed, the girl's face and hands were a dusky blue. Her mother was nearly paralyzed with fear.

You can take too much of some medicines and come out of it just fine. The body will tolerate high levels of certain chemicals. Sometimes, the medicine is not well absorbed; other times, it might not affect critical body functions. You can take, say, too many stool softeners and end up with lots of very soft stool but no toxicity.

But there is another group of medicines in which taking even a little bit more than the prescribed dose will have awful consequences. For these medicines, the therapeutic window between a dose high enough to be effective and one that is toxic is tiny. These are the drugs imprinted on every emergency doctor's mind. Most overdoses don't have big consequences; there is often nothing to be done other than to get an understanding of how and why the overdose happened to prevent it from happening again. But we doctors truly shudder when we hear about overdoses of certain medicines: children taking iron tablets, an overdose of Aspirin, or an overdose of many diabetes medicines. These will all smoothly kill a person. I've seen patients die in front of my eyes soon after taking large doses of blood pressure medicine. The drugs go to work on the heart and arteries and veins, and they do what they are supposed to do, with no endpoint other than their own declining concentration. The drugs themselves overwhelm any treatment we can provide. They relentlessly affect the intimate and critical human systems that keep us alive. These overdose patients die with surprised looks on their faces as their blood pressure falls to zero and their vision goes black, and they deflate as if they were punctured air mattresses.

As dangerous as these medicines are, at the cellular and pharmacologic level, such powerful drugs all have a certain elegance. The way they work explains their utility, and it also predicts the effects of taking too much. Their mechanisms predict their antidotes.

The drug our teenager had swallowed was an elegant but terrible medicine. Isoniazid, known in short form as INH, is an antibiotic that inhibits the cell wall growth of mycobacteria like tuberculosis. It is not one that we commonly see in the West. But it's a useful treatment throughout Africa, where TB remains a real problem.

To me, this overdose was uniquely interesting, if very dangerous. It was like finding an exotic toxic flower in a foreign land. Isoniazid overdose is one of those things that every medical student has permanently stored in their mind. It's part of a list of causes for unexplained acidosis of the blood that we're all forced to memorize when we're in training.

The human body is pretty good at maintaining a constant pH, the balance between acids and bases in the body. When the blood becomes too acidic, causes are broadly categorized as either respiratory acidosis or metabolic acidosis. Knowing the difference is critical for understanding how to fix things. Respiratory acidosis occurs when a body retains too much carbon dioxide, usually due to failed breathing. Alternatively, acidosis can also be caused by certain body metabolites released into the blood, or by kidney problems leading to the body's inability to hold onto base. Doctors will narrow the metabolic acidosis differential by determining whether acidosis is caused by the respiratory system. If not, we will look for something called an anion gap. Only a limited number of causes of metabolic acidosis have an increased anion gap, so these steps are helpful in coming to a diagnosis.

When we were medical students taking a written test, we all wrote the acronym MUDPILES in the margin of our test book to remind ourselves of the causes of anion gap metabolic acidosis. MUDPILES describes the common causes of anion gap acidosis. It stands for Methanol, Uremia, Diabetic ketoacidosis, Paraldehyde, Isoniazid, Lactic acidosis, Ethylene glycol, and Salicylates.

Over the course of a career, a practicing doctor will likely see many of the causes of anion gap metabolic acidosis on that list. Diabetes and uremia are daily culprits in most emergency departments. Methanol and

Ethylene glycol ingestions are typically annual events; they create terrible poisonings from drinking moonshine and antifreeze and cause blindness and kidney failure. But there are two drugs on the list that I'd bet no doctor that I'd worked with had ever seen in clinical practice: an overdose of the ancient and never-seen paraldehyde ("P"), an old-fashioned and unpleasant sedative that had long since been replaced by safer and better tolerated medicines, and an overdose of isoniazid ("I").

Doctors today still use medical knowledge gleaned hundreds of years ago and subsequently passed from generation to generation. The era of scientific medicine arguably began around the beginning of the nineteenth century. The fields of physiology, pharmacology, microscopy, and pathology were advancing rapidly then, and the body's functions were coming to be scientifically understood. Doctors in those years developed standard curricula which they taught to their pupils. Over time, incrementally, older information gets discarded, and new information gets added. But because this is an iterative process and science progresses only so quickly, a lot of the information that was first taught to doctors in the early nineteenth century remains in our textbooks and is still taught today.

Since 1952, at least, doctors have understood and taught the consequences of an isoniazid overdose. The first antibiotics were discovered in the 1930s. The first anti-tuberculosis antibiotic, streptomycin, was discovered in 1944, followed by isoniazid in 1952. By 2008, I was unlikely to ever see either paraldehyde or isoniazid in Western practice—but those drugs had remained on our board exams. It was great luck that they had, because here we were, on our way to a remote part of Africa to treat a case of isoniazid overdose.

At noon, John and I were supposed to have been in the Citation jet bound for Tanzania, but instead we were fidgeting planeside at Wilson, waiting for an ambulance to bring one of the nurses back from a nearby pharmacy. We needed large doses of the INH antidote, which wasn't something we carried in our drug bag. There was no sense in leaving without it, because the girl's seizures would likely continue until the antidote was given. We would waste time leaving without it. It was better to wait.

The antidote we needed was a simple vitamin, B6, given in large doses. INH's metabolic pathway can explain this unlikely solution: INH has an affinity for, and binds to, vitamin B6 (pyridoxine) in the blood, making it unavailable for other uses. B6 is needed by the body to make a range of proteins, including the synaptic neurotransmitters found in the brain, such as GABA, a neurotransmitter which serves to "calm" neurons. GABA is a neurotransmitter affected by alcohol and sedatives such as Valium; INH's affinity for B6 effectively makes it an "anti-Valium," causing neuronal excitement.

And that's exactly what happened. After our patient took a large dose of INH, her decreased levels of B6 led to a sharp drop in her brain's GABA. Without enough GABA, she convulsed, and her blood filled with acid generated by her seizures. INH-induced seizures are remarkably hard to stop; the usual medications, anticonvulsants such as Valium or valproic acid, don't work well. What's really needed to reverse the seizures is simply a replenishment of B6. But time is of the essence. Seizures need to be stopped as quickly as possible; every minute the brain is in an electrical storm, it is being damaged. Extended seizures can cause long-term brain damage.

Time dragged, but finally, within a few minutes of our scheduled takeoff, a Flying Doctors ambulance pulled past the hangar gate and onto the tarmac with its lights flashing. The nurse handed us a hand-labeled plastic bag with small tablets of B6 inside. She explained that there was no intravenous B6 to be found on short notice, but a pharmacist in Nairobi had rummaged around and found a handful of B6 tablets in the back. They came in a big bottle and cost pennies each, their low price belying their value. We would make do. They would save a life.

In the air, John and I discussed our steps. We imagined the girl in bad shape, wracked with seizures, unable to keep her throat open and clear of secretions. We would need to sedate and then intubate her, and put a nasogastric tube in her nose, down her throat, and into her stomach. We would load her with a benzodiazepine. John would crush the B6 tablets and add some water, and we would use a big syringe to push the crushed tablets into her stomach. It was a crude approach. There was no guarantee that the seizing girl would digest the tablets—with her adrenalin surge, blood flow to the stomach had likely decreased. Because we'd be sedating and paralyzing her to gain control of her airway, we would, for some time, have no idea whether her seizures were continuing; her brain might be convulsed by an electrical storm of activity while her muscles were silent. But, without taking control of her airway before filling her stomach with fluid and tablets, we risked disaster.

We entered Tanzanian airspace and began to

descend. The pilots landed smoothly and taxied and parked. Carrying our airway and medication bags, John and I walked over to a UN ambulance that had pulled up by our wing. I opened the side door to the ambulance, expecting bodies hunched over the stretcher furiously working on the patient—the scene that typically signaled the fierce attention of a medical team fighting for a life. But this time, there was only silence. An attendant sat expressionless on the bench seat, holding a clipboard and a stack of papers. My eyes went to the shape under a sheet, head tilted away from us, unmoving, no longer convulsing. For a moment, I was sure that we had been too late.

A middle-aged, handsome woman sat next to the cot. She had pursed lips and a taut face, and she refused to look at us. She turned to the stretcher and spoke in short, clipped sentences. Her daughter, whose face was tear-streaked and largely expressionless, turned to us. She was groggy but able to answer questions. Her competence was completely unexpected. For reasons probably tied to the size of the dose she had taken, her body, on its own, had begun to metabolize the INH and produce GABA once again. Her seizures had stopped without treatment.

Moving the girl and her mother onto the plane, we headed for Nairobi. Over the next hour, we flew mostly in silence. John held a can of juice and a straw, and he fed our fragile young patient one tablet of B6 at a time. I remember that her mother looked straight ahead for the entire flight, vacant, even callous, as tears fell from her daughter's eyes.

People rarely become hysterical when tragedy strikes, and they never get slapped as they do in the movies. Most people in the early stages of absorbing tragedy are slow to react; they are, psychically and physically, in a temporary state of suspended animation. Mostly, they are unable to keep up. Their psyches are protecting them from absorbing too much, too fast, acting as a circuit breaker of sorts. Looking across the cabin, I recognized the patient's mother as someone living perhaps the worst day of her life. She was simply unable to engage with the world. The mother's unusual behavior was a coping mechanism.

So, none of us spoke much. We sipped water, and did paperwork, and monitored the girl as she snored in a post-seizure deep slumber. But mostly, we looked out the window at the passing Rift Valley below, stunned and relieved. All of us were acutely aware that a young woman had nearly died in a terrible way. Her salvation came from a medical factoid nearly sixty years old, a clinical afterthought that had yet to be purged from the textbooks and one that was still taught to generations of medical students, me included.

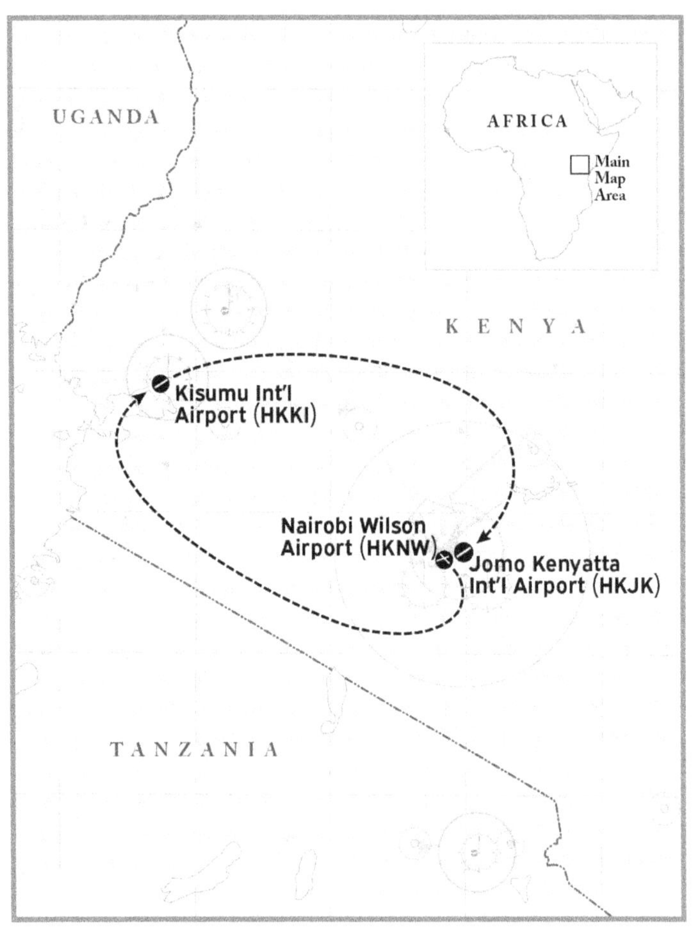

Evacuation from Kisumu, Kenya, using a King Air

THROWING STARS

The star thrower is a man, and death is running more fleet than he along every seabeach in the world.

— Loren Eiseley, *The Star Thrower*

Operations called me after dinner. There was a flight planned for the following morning to Kisumu, which was located in Kenya, northwest of Nairobi, on Lake Victoria. The patient was a young man who was suffering from delirium and needed to be transferred to Nairobi. Like usual, we'd leave at first light.

Then my Nokia rang again: I was told that we needed to leave immediately. A taxi was on the way to the Club to pick me up. This was highly unusual. We'd already had a long day of flying, two different rescues, and I was looking forward to a drink and my hard bed. But instead, I rooted in the back of my closet for a clean uniform shirt and pulled on a fresh pair of socks and my boots. It was going to be a long night.

Night flying is unusual in Africa. The pilots can't land at most airports at night because there are few lit runways across the continent, and landing in the bush on a dark field would be too risky. Kisumu, where we were headed, was one of the few airports that could accommodate a landing after dusk.

Michael and I packed our medical equipment into the back of the plane and got onboard a twin-prop for the forty-five-minute flight. We took off in the dark and landed in Kisumu around nine. From the cockpit, the captain told us that the runway lights were normally turned off after eight. It seemed that somebody had twisted somebody else's arm to accommodate our late arrival and even later departure. One way or the other, he said, we needed to be gone by midnight.

A dented van met us planeside. It was an old secondhand ambulance; its shelves were empty and labeled with engraved plastic plaques in Korean. It was clearly a donation from a government aid agency. We stacked our equipment on the ambulance's gurney: a ventilator, oxygen, medical bags. And then we set off for the Kisumu regional hospital, a painful forty-five-minute drive across potholed dirt roads through shanty towns devoid of light. In the back of the ambulance, we were tossed about wildly. We tried to brace ourselves with our feet as the van bounced into deep ruts and the driver fought to drive back out of them. But we were mostly at the mercy of the roads.

As we rode, the headlights would illuminate movement in front of the huts and corrugated iron shacks. I realized that entire families had streamed out of their homes to watch us drive by; few people were asleep.

The hospital was in town and marked by a simple, painted wooden sign next to the road. It had a large gate which a guard opened. We pulled into an empty dirt lot and stopped in front of a mildew-stained rectangle of concrete illuminated by one incandescent bulb above the entrance. As it was late, few rooms were lit, and there was only a skeleton crew around, including the night watchmen who held the keys to the barred gates that barricaded the entrances to the hallways. The gates were to keep thieves from stealing from sleeping patients in the middle of the night once their families left for home.

Michael rang the doorbell and banged on the glass, hoping to rouse an escort— anyone. Eventually, a tired nurse looked through the window and then unlocked the door to the emergency room. A guard, sprawled in a white plastic chair, pointed the way. Once we passed into the corridor, the hospital quickly became a dark and frightening place. The staff had turned off the lights to save energy, and the pitted concrete corridors were covered with puddles of water. Several times, at the ends of long corridors, we reached a locked set of bars and were forced to turn around. Finally, after another dead-end, Michael yelled down the hall. There was a shuffle, the sound of something dropping. A thin night watchman lazily approached us from the opposite side of the gate to let us into the ward. He'd been sleeping on a plastic chair in the corner. Michael, normally a decent-natured, if wry, fellow, was by this point covered in sweat and quite unhappy. He yelled again, which caused the small man to fumble the key. After opening the gate, he gave us all a wide berth.

Michael, I would learn, was not to be messed with. He had studied nursing at the Kenya Medical Training College in Nairobi and had become an extraordinary bedside nurse. His talent had been recognized by the leadership at AMREF, and he landed a coveted spot at the service. AMREF was known for hiring the best nurses in Kenya; they provided good pay and top-quality continuing education, which kept their nurses from leaving for the UK and Europe for work, a common path for well-trained but miserably underpaid Kenyan nurses.

Michael had been at Flying Doctors forever—which is to say that he had seen it all. That night, he was not in the mood for nonsense on a mission that was already off- kilter. A young overnight nurse dressed in a starched light blue smock, cap, and white shoes saw us enter the ward. Catching Michael's eye, she pointed to a bed at the far end of the room, which was a long hall shared by nine other patients and two nurses. There, a young Kenyan man lay unconscious on an uncovered plastic mattress. He was thin, with curly, dark hair, and a blank, empty gaze. He lay on his side, his head propped up with a blanket roll and tilted so saliva poured from his mouth, dripping first onto the plastic and then pooling under his chest. I could hear his ragged breathing as he struggled for air.

His mother, who stood at the head of the bed holding her son's head, was a plump, taciturn woman wearing a flowing, vibrantly printed dress and head wrap. In her face, I could read relief, arrogance, and defensiveness. She was frightened, but perhaps also relieved to see us. Her son, Ephraim, was twenty. They had brought him to the hospital after he came down with a fever and a severe headache a few days earlier. In the ED, the doctors examined him and came up with a diagnostic plan. As is typical in most African hospitals, they family would need to purchase supplies and medications from one of the several brightly lit pharmacies down the block and bring them back to the hospital. Sure enough, the hospital sent the family out with a shopping list of medical supplies: a spinal needle, sterile gloves, IV fluids, and antibiotics. The family returned clutching these supplies in a paper sack. The doctor then put the needle into the febrile man's back, threading it through his vertebrae until he felt a pop. A cloudy stream of cerebrospinal fluid shot from the needle, under pressure, across the bed before the doctor could adjust the stream into a test tube. Something was causing an increase in the pressure of the fluid around Ephraim's brain. It was most likely an infection.

The overnight doctor was a young man with a shiny face, wearing a starched white coat and open dress shirt. He arrived looking exhausted. We made our introductions, and he handed me the sealed envelope containing Ephraim's medical records. The tests were back from the lumbar puncture, he said. The white cells were high; the sugar and protein in the cerebrospinal fluid, both markers of infection, were wildly off. There were four types of infection possible in a young man in Kenya: malaria, a leading cause of illness in Africa; bacterial meningitis caused by Neisseria bacteria, which was common across Africa's dusty "meningitis belt" that stretched from the Atlantic across the continent; tuberculosis, which was an endemic risk; or some type of virus. The organism invading Ephraim's brain would determine the therapy and, really, the outcome. Standing around Ephraim's bedside, all of us experienced a momentary ping of selfish concern. We were vulnerable, too. Neisseria was quite transmissible.

Yet, there was something else going on. I could sense it, but I couldn't put my finger on what it was. The doctor seemed uncomfortable. He bounced from foot to foot and answered my questions in single sentences. Ephraim's mother, too, who had stopped holding her son's head, was acting strangely. She now stood by the bed, arms crossed like a crossing guard, glaring at the doctor when he spoke. It occurred to me that she didn't want others to hear what the doctor was saying. The room was full; there would be few confidences in this space. In unison, we lowered our voices. The doctor, who was standing right next to me, leaned over and whispered in my ear:

"It is likely Cryptococcus."

He stepped away. And then I understood. I could see in my mind the Cryptococcus fungus under a microscope, looking like perfect Olympic rings (Cryptococcus means "hidden sphere" in Greek). The fungus was the key to the story.

Healthy Africans could become infected with Cryptococcus, but such infections weren't common. What I now knew to be true—what suddenly had been revealed, what nobody wanted to say out loud—was that Ephraim, the thin, young man who struggled to breathe beside us, probably had AIDS. He was dying from an opportunistic infection.

That was the secret. *That* was the cause for the mother's defiance and for her willingness to protect her son from the diseases that were killing him and the rumors that would destroy him.

I also understood that the narrative of our emergency flight here was more complicated than it had initially seemed. Our entire trip had been choreographed by powers that could make things happen. A politician or a businessman—someone with influence—had intervened. It would explain our unusual late-night travel, the airport lights, the bashful doctor, and the well-dressed mother, whose son who wouldn't spend a minute more in Kisumu than was absolutely necessary. In the way Africa works, totally opaque to me, someone had caused the gears to turn. I, an oblivious but well-meaning cog, would pluck Ephraim from a ward where eight other equally sick Africans suffered in anonymity.

And that's how it all came together.

The more time I spent in Africa, the more I realized that when I took a call, I was not some observer who could watch from afar, like an anthropologist in a camouflaged hut observing lives unfold. I was part of the scene, filling the role of the benevolent white doctor. Everyone around me had seen people like me before; I was not an unknown to them. But it was all new to me.

At that moment, all I understood was that my role in this particular piece of theater was to stabilize this man and bring him to safety. We never mentioned his secret again. The doctor sealed the envelope that contained his medical records, and we stuck it beneath the mattress on the gurney.

I looked at Ephraim and knew that we needed to escalate care. Hospitals in Africa tended to have a high threshold for putting in breathing tubes. Once a patient had a breathing tube, it had to be connected to a scarce ventilator or else to a dedicated family member who would need to squeeze a respiratory bag mask every few seconds, twenty-four hours a day. The hospitals would intervene aggressively with patients who had stopped breathing, but not necessarily with those who were only struggling to breathe or who were at risk of aspirating their secretions. It was a problem of scarcity and limited assets.

We couldn't transport Ephraim with an unsecured airway. Aspirating his secretions would give him a severe pneumonia, and vomit during the flight could easily obstruct his airway. His respirations were inadequate, as well; we needed to support his breathing.

I told Michael what we had to do: put a tube into Ephraim's trachea, stick him on a ventilator, and run. It wasn't safe any other way. Michael nodded and opened the drug bag. He pulled up glass vials and checked and cross-checked them, and then he got the drugs ready. We would use a sedative and a muscle paralytic, which would allow us to place a breathing tube in Ephraim's trachea and take over his breathing. I prepared the vent tubing and the airway kit, getting the laryngoscope and the tube ready. Michael went to start fresh IVs, but the young man's body was swollen from infection. Only after trying three or four times did Michael find a vein—a tiny one, on our patient's foot.

We were ready. Watched intently by the other eight patients in the room, Michael pushed the medications, one after the other, through the tiny foot vein. I could see Ephraim's jaw and neck go flaccid; then his breaths slowed, and then they stopped.

There is something sublime about having used your hands so many times to do something that they can almost function by themselves. I've felt this sensation of letting my hands move automatically while making clay pots on a wheel. And I feel it when I intubate. It's a tricky skill and is far more nuanced that it might seem. Every person's body is slightly different; the tissues feel a certain way, or the tongue is floppy, or the jaw is heavy, or the neck is skinny, or the landmarks are close together. As a doctor, I had intubated patients hundreds of times. I had been confronted with every physical variation there was, and I had worked through all of them until I could intubate skillfully, even in the worst of circumstances. Even in this dark ward in Africa.

Placing myself at the head of Ephraim's bed, I bent down and looked into his mouth. I could, at first, see nothing but swollen tissue and frothy saliva. The room was dark, and the light from the laryngoscope was meager. I suctioned with our aspirator, hard, and for a moment I could see where I needed to be. My hands moved with smooth, practiced motion: left hand pulling up on the laryngoscope, right hand on the tube at the corner of the mouth, then a spiral turn to the cords, and *in*. Then pulling the laryngoscope out and pushing it into the mattress to close its hinge and shut off its light, my right hand never letting go of the tube, my left hand next inflating the cuff with a syringe. Michael was ready with strong tape to secure it in place.

We connected Ephraim to the ventilator, and the machine began to rhythmically push air into his lungs every few seconds. On our monitor, I could see a sawtooth tracing showing that Ephraim was exhaling the built-up CO2 in his system. With every breath, his numbers improved.

It was time to move. The pilot had called my cell phone a few times, but I couldn't pick up. He rang a third time, and I lifted the phone to my ear. He sounded unusually edgy; the controller in the tower was threatening to close the airport if we waited any longer. If that happened, we would be stuck in Kisumu for the night.

Michael and I grabbed Ephraim under his arms and legs and swung him onto the stretcher. We piled our monitor, the oxygen tank, and our three medical equipment bags onto his legs. Then, trailed by his mother, we wheeled Ephraim down the ward, past the other patients and toward the door. Speed-walking, we raced along wet hallways, steered around puddles, and then pushed through the main doors of the hospital and into much cooler air. Ephraim lay unconscious on the gurney. His ventilator had started to flash and beep; it needed to be plugged in and the battery switched.

Ephraim's mother sat in the passenger seat of the ambulance, while Michael and I sat in the back in the dark silence, waiting for the driver to start the engine. The ventilator provided a dim light. Every few seconds, the vent would trigger, and air would be pushed into Ephraim's lungs. The monitor continued to alarm: low battery. The driver slammed the back hatch door shut and jumped into the driver's seat, banging his door. He turned the key. Nothing. Just the unmistakable click of a dead battery. I stared at Michael. Holy shit.

Michael, to his credit, looked only mildly bothered. Leaving me in the back, he exited the van and, with the two guards he had summoned from the guard shack, rocked, then pushed the van through the dark lot, ultimately at a jogging pace. The driver was able to pop the clutch, and the engine came to life. The small roof light in the back came on. Soon, with red emergency lights illuminating the roadway, we pulled through the gate and began our return across the rutted roads and potholes. Almost immediately, medical bags, pieces of equipment, and discarded medical packaging began rolling back and forth across the floor of the van. Ephraim remained still, tethered to the stretcher, his critical endotracheal tube taped to his face.

As we passed through village after village, shanty dogs barked at the groaning van. The captain had seen our flashing red lights coming down a hill a mile away and had already done the pre-flight checks. It was nearly midnight. The tower was closing; the controller really was done with us. The moment the van stopped, we flung open the doors and grabbed the stretcher. Along with the driver and pilots, we carried Ephraim, a cocooned silent mass, into the plane. Michael and I quickly rifled through our bags for new batteries and switched the emptied oxygen tank to the airplanes' installed supply.

The engine's starter clicked like the ignitor on a gas stove, and the turbines whined to life, one after the other. The plane started moving at a good clip, even as the copilot closed and secured the door. We knelt on the floor trying to brace everything as we taxied, fast, to the end of the runway. With a hard right swing, and without slowing, the plane powered to full throttle, and we accelerated down the runway. I held an IV bag and watched as the cardiac monitor went wild with the vibration and movement of the plane. From the side windows, I could see the runway lights shut off seconds after our tires left the asphalt.

My pants stuck to my legs with sweat, and my armpits and chest were soaked. I wiped my face with a paper towel and greedily drank some cool water. We ascended and headed for Nairobi—Michael and I; our two pilots; a taciturn mother; and a young, sick, unconscious Kenyan patient.

Once on the ground at the international airport—Wilson had closed for the night— we loaded Ephraim into an ambulance and drove through empty streets to Kenya's public referral hospital, a hulking concrete box called Kenyatta National Hospital. At eighteen hundred beds, Kenyatta was the largest referral hospital in the country. It had an open-door policy, which meant that there could be more patients than beds— sometimes thousands more. Kenyatta was a frequent target of abuse in the local papers, but the truth remained that, like all public hospitals the world over, it was essential to Kenya and its people.

Once in the hospital, we wheeled Ephraim to an elevator and then to the intensive care unit. There, a physician resident came to collect our papers and get a clinical report. Michael, who knew Kenyatta intimately, knew where to find a spare ventilator and rummaged around until he found one. Together, Michael and I ensured that the new ventilator had been properly attached to the breathing tube.

And that was that.

In the middle of the night, with Ephraim safely delivered to Kenyatta, our duties were over. We disconnected Ephraim from our equipment, made sure that there was still sedative left in the IV bag, and found our way out of the hospital. None of us would ever hear of Ephraim again. All we could do was leave him in capable hands and hope that our efforts had made a difference.

Seated in the AMREF ambulance once again, as Pato steered us through quiet streets back to Wilson, I reflected on our heroic trip, on our multi-million-dollar plane filled with world-class critical care equipment. I wondered if we were spending money the right way. I wondered if saving one life at a time in a health care desert was the highest moral use of our talents and resources. My team and I would frequently evacuate patients from one awful hospital in East Africa, provide them with American-standard care in the air, and then deposit them at a second awful hospital. The discrepancies only worsened when we were bringing charity cases from the outer reaches of East Africa to the city.

That was our brief: stabilize the patient, then transport them to one of Nairobi's hospitals. The questions assailed me for my entire sojourn in Kenya. Was there value in saving one life when we left dozens of equally sick, but less fortunate, people behind? Would it be better to dispense with the air rescues and use the money to buy cheap vaccines for hundreds or thousands of kids? Which moral framework would we use to justify our choices, and who would make the decision?

Chopping a tall poppy wouldn't make the situation at African rural hospitals any better, especially since the biggest issues in African health care seem to stem as much from problems with execution and leadership as from an absolute lack of money. The bigger truth was that for the person who was dying in a dusty town or dirty hospital, who witnessed our plane circling a dirt runway, and who was lifted from the floor of a van and packed aboard our flight, the issue was academic.

> *Along the strip of wet sand that marks the ebbing and flowing of the tide, death walks hugely and in many forms...*

I was reminded of Loren Eisley's famous short story about sea life suffocating on a beach at low tide. One starfish, among a holocaust of dying animals, raised its arm, begging to be saved from the mud. The star thrower threw it into deep water. Did it make a difference in the scheme of things? To that starfish, yes.

I wasn't a politician or a World Bank executive or a bioethicist. Nor did I have the temperament to be an aid worker working under the most difficult of conditions, bless them. I could turn away, discouraged by the futility of saving one life amid the terrible carnage caused by malaria, HIV, violent deaths, and starvation in East Africa. Or I could choose simply to engage, to do the very best I could for one patient at a time. And that was enough for me. There was nothing conceptual about an improbable complex rescue from the bush. What a tangible miracle to have your life saved. Nothing could matter more to you and to those who love you.

> *I had seen the rainbow attempting to attach itself to earth. On a point of land, as though projecting into a domain beyond us, I found the star thrower. In the sweet rain-swept morning, that great many-hued rain-bow still lurked and wavered tentatively beyond him. Silently I sought and picked up a still-living star, spinning it far out into the waves. I spoke once briefly. "I understand," I said. "Call me another thrower." Only then I allowed myself to think, He is not alone any longer. After us there will be others. We were part of the rainbow.*

I was throwing stars, I realized. Making a difference to just one was enough.

SECTION 2: LONG RAIN SEASON, 2012

All journeys have secret destinations
of which the traveler is unaware.

- Martin Buber

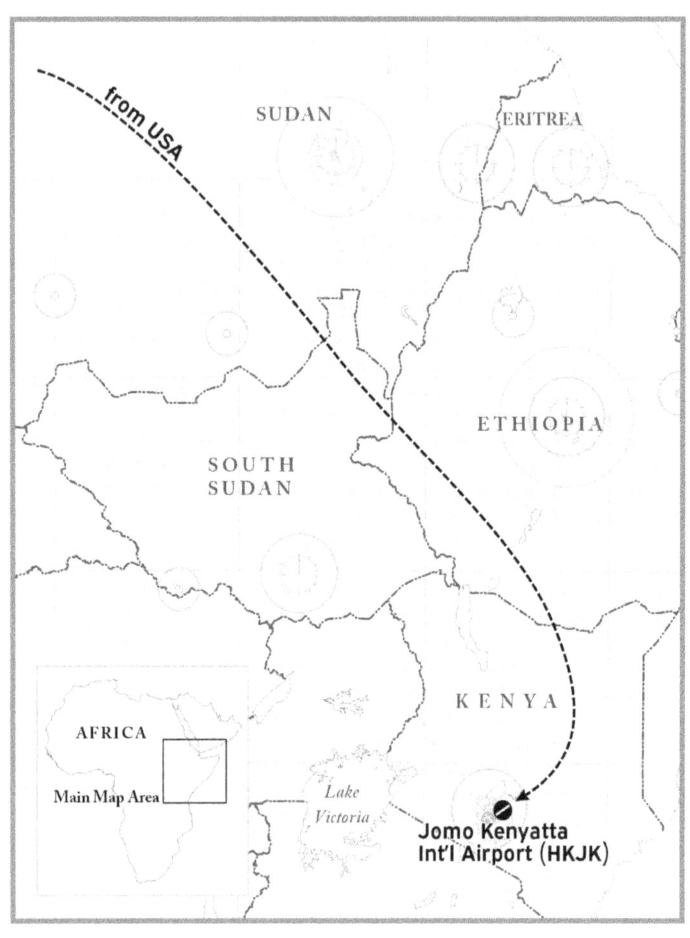
from USA
SUDAN
ERITREA
ETHIOPIA
SOUTH
SUDAN
KENYA
AFRICA
Main Map Area
Lake
Victoria
Jomo Kenyatta
Int'l Airport (HKJK)

AN AGENT IN THE CHAOS

Prevented by the duties of life on the surface from looking down into the depths, yet all the while being slowly trained by them to descend as a shaping agent into the chaos, whence the fragrance of white wintergreen bears the promise of a new belonging. At the frontier—

- Dag Hammarskjöld,
second Secretary-General of the UN

Four years had passed since my sojourn in Nairobi. Superficially, the place looked the same. The airport's international terminal, which had been constructed in the 1960s during the heyday of African independence, looked as tired and beleaguered as it had when I last saw it. There was a sense of timelessness to the place—the same duty-free shops, the same imported alcohol and tobacco cartons, the same crummy African crafts made in China.

But looks could be deceptive; much had changed. Now, teams of heavily armed Kenyan police and soldiers patrolled the airport. Their presence confirmed the news coming out of the country: Kenya was on a war footing. The national mood, the economy, and the day-to-day life of every Kenyan had been affected. For the next month, I would be conscripted into that sweep of affairs.

The origins of this trouble lay next door in Somalia. In 2008, as I was leaving my first rotation with Flying Doctors, Somalia's degeneration into chaos had accelerated. An al-Qaeda affiliate group, al-Shabaab, meaning "the youth" in Arabic, had become a significant nationalist and jihadist force in that country. In the face of a collapsed economy and deepening hunger, the Islamists in the south and central parts of Somalia had gained support from average Somalis. The Islamists were powerful, unified, vicious, and deadly—and they sought to overthrow the fragile Somali government. The African Union forces, which included Kenyan troops, and which had support from the West, put boots on the ground in Somalia. They were trying to keep ideology and instability from spreading across borders into Kenya, Ethiopia, and Uganda by fighting al-Shabaab directly in the streets.

In September 2011, a few months before I returned to Africa, there was a significant escalation in terrorism. A British couple on holiday had been kidnapped from their hotel room near Lamu by al-Shabaab. The husband was murdered, and his wife was taken hostage and brought to Somalia where she was held captive for seven months. A month later, gunmen kidnapped a disabled French woman. She died in captivity.

These kidnappings triggered the launch of Operation Linda Nchi ("protect the country") by Kenya's military, aimed at creating a buffer zone along Kenya's northeastern border. Al-Shabaab responded with a series of bomb attacks in the markets and random attacks at shopping centers in Kenya. Jihad had a massive effect on Kenya: the violence destabilized the tourist industry and economy. The al-Shabaab violence would crescendo in a large-scale terrorist attack at a Nairobi mall in 2013, which killed dozens, and a mass shooting at a university in 2015.

It's hard to overstate the psychological effect that al-Shabaab had on East Africans. Tourism fell, average Kenyans became too frightened to go outside, and the TV news spent hours discussing terrorism. Public confidence was undermined, and there were worries that the East African governments weren't equipped or prepared to fight the insurgents, who were unconstrained by the porous borders. Kenya, it turned out, was experiencing a slow-motion version of America's 9/11. The terrorists had captured the national imagination—and, through terror, the country.

Against this backdrop, I wondered what I was doing back in East Africa. What was it that had brought me back after four years away, especially to this environment of fear? I tried to articulate to my wife, fully, why I needed to go. We were newlyweds, just exiting the honeymoon phase. She was coming to terms with my wanderlust (this was before she learned to shrug and say "fine" to my travel schemes). For me, the stakes were higher; there was now someone at home who wanted me kept safe.

I explained to her—superficially—that if I passed on this opportunity, I would never return. Entanglements and dependence don't decrease in middle age; I would soon be unable to manage a month away from home or, in good conscience, to expose myself to such risks. The honest truth was that I was still searching.

In my time away, I had made some progress in understanding why Africa had become such a preoccupation for me. I found insights in an unusual book of meditations and poetry written by a diplomat named Dag Hammarskjöld. His book, *Markings,* was an esoteric book, a serendipitous find. Hammarskjöld was the second secretary-general of the United Nations, appointed not long after the UN was formed from the ashes of World War II. He spent significant time in Africa doing peacekeeping work and, in 1961, was on his way to ceasefire negotiations during the Congo Crisis when his DC-6 unexpectedly crashed in Zambia, killing everyone on board. It was most likely shot down; after all these years, sordid details still emerge.

Hammarskjöld had kept an extensive diary documenting his inner world before and during his time with the UN. *Markings* was published after his death. In the book, Hammarskjöld strangely made no reference to his daily work as a diplomat—though WH Auden, who was a friend of Hammarskjöld and who wrote the introduction to the book, stressed the inseparability of Hammarskjöld's inner world and his work. *Markings*, he wrote, was “the attempt by a professional man of action to unite in one life the *via activa* and the *via contemplativa*.” It was the secretary-general’s attempt to understand his own essence and motivations— the reasons he worked long hours in dangerous places. It was an attempt to derive purpose from his work. It was the same search I was on.

Auden wrote:

> *...any "discovery" we make about ourselves or the meaning of life is never, like a scientific discovery, a coming upon something entirely new and unsuspected: It is, rather, the coming to conscious recognition of something which we really knew all the time, but, because we were unwilling or unable to formulate it correctly, we did not hitherto know we knew.*

For Hammarskjöld, self-knowledge and understanding demanded exposure to the unknown, to the frontiers of his daily existence. He aimed to experience their mystery and ignore superficial, inconsequential things. Hammarskjöld knew, deeply, that he was doing the work he was destined to do by opening himself to the profound mysteries of life, those hidden places. Looking into the depths trained him to become an "agent in the chaos," a public servant of the highest level. The rest, for him, was noise.

It was then that I understood why reaching these frontiers in Africa mattered to me. I wondered if my exposure to new frontiers beyond my daily existence placed my purpose and role into better perspective. Maybe these frontiers, no matter how violent or complex, provided a window into my own values and motivations. If I were fully honest with myself (and my anxious spouse), the increasing troubles and complexity in East Africa fascinated and frightened me, and they drew me in. I didn't see the evolving Jihadi crisis in East Africa as a reason to stay away. I saw it as something to know and to understand—if that could be done. Being in East Africa could teach me a lot.

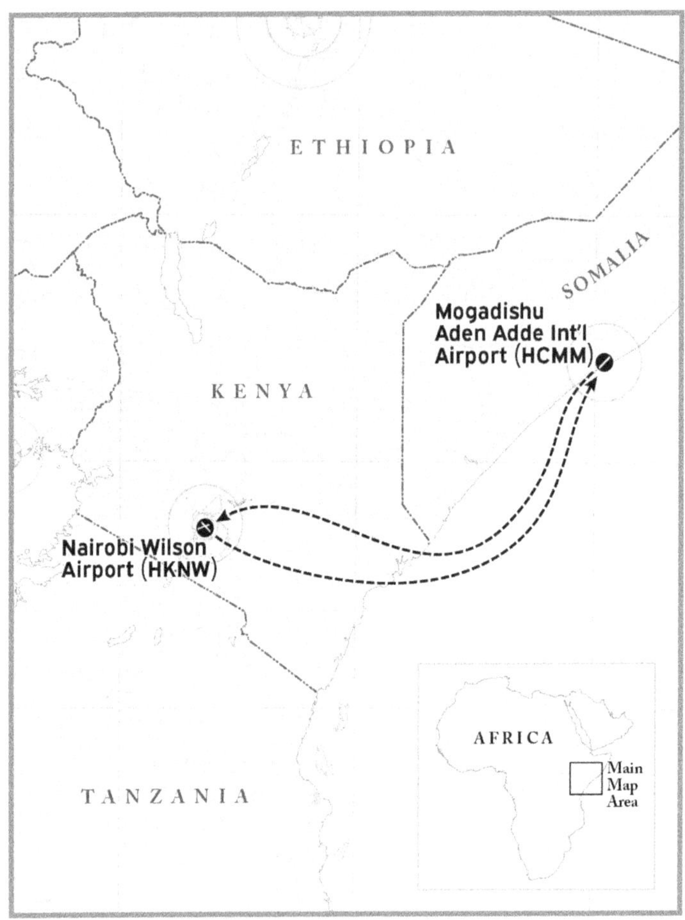

Evacuation from Mogadishu, Somalia, using a Citation

SHOOTING STRANGERS

"It is not fickle, but because it has mothered not only men, but races, and cradled not only cities, but civilizations — and seen them die, and seen new ones born again — Africa can be dispassionate, indifferent, warm, or cynical, replete with the weariness of too much wisdom."

— Beryl Markham

Like my arrival in 2008, I was again picked up at the airport by Pato—but this time, under the watchful eyes of heavily armed police officers overseeing the road outside arrivals. Pato dropped me at the Aero Club, which, despite the troubles in Kenya, seemed the same as ever. The rooms were visibly dustier than before, but someone had fixed the poor water pressure, and a new chef had made the effort to update the menu. The changes seemed like the kind that would be orchestrated by a niece intervening to tidy up her aunt's flowered sitting room; they were welcome, but token in the scheme of things.

Before he left, Pato had handed me a mobile phone to keep. He warned me that we'd have a flight in the morning. Predictably, within minutes, the control desk at Wilson called. We would head directly northeast, into the heart of the violence, in the morning.

The task was not uncomplicated. We were to fly an unarmed, unescorted air ambulance two hundred miles up the coast of Somalia, over al-Shabaab territory, and aim for the only dot of land that was then under Somali federal control at that time: the city of Mogadishu proper. There were no safe contingency airports anywhere between Kenya's northeast provinces and Mogadishu. Once we passed Ras Kamboni, the southernmost city in Somalia, which sits on the Kenyan border, we would be in no-man's land. In the event of a mechanical emergency, our rescue mission would itself require a rescue coordinated at the highest levels. We would likely become an international crisis.

If I needed a reminder of the dangers of kidnappers,

six months earlier, there had been a dramatic rescue of a captured American near Galkayo, Somalia. In late 2011, Jessica Buchanan, a 32-year-old American teacher, and Poul Thisted, a Danish national, were captured by Somali pirates and held hostage for a forty-five-million-dollar ransom. Both Buchanan and Thisted were NGO workers whose SUV was held up at gunpoint. Buchanan was in Somalia to train children on how to avoid landmines; she had sold her belongings to become a missionary in Africa and had spent years in East Africa as a teacher.

For three months, the Somali captors denied the hostages access to adequate food, water, and medicine. Buchanan's health gradually deteriorated. The pirates eventually turned down a final ransom offer. By then, Buchanan was near death. On the night of President Obama's 2012 State of the Union address, SEAL Team 6 parachuted into the Somali countryside, raided the camp, shot the captors, and rescued the two hostages. There is an iconic photo of President Obama in the Capitol on the phone with Buchanan's father letting him know of the rescue. Taken only a few months before our flight to Somalia, it was a reminder of the consequences of getting things wrong. Accidental infections, rare African viruses, needlesticks, corrupt officials, bad roads, and bad weather were no longer my biggest concerns.

I arrived early the next morning at Wilson, and we loaded the jet the same way as before. I quickly reviewed the drug bags and equipment, noting what had been changed and which medications had been added. Then, once again, I climbed into the back of the AMREF jet, this time with Lillian, a new nurse I hadn't worked with before. We flew east, toward Mogadishu. We'd been called to collect three wounded African Union soldiers and bring them to Kenya.

After hugging the Kenyan coast, the plane crossed the air border into Somalia, a slightly anticlimactic event. You might imagine, from what you see in movies and hear on the news, that Somalia is an ugly, desperate place. In fact, the Somali coast looked idyllic, an unspoiled Maldives, with miles of untouched soft sand beaches reaching out into blue Indian Ocean water and the occasional fishing village. Staring out the airplane window onto what was likely the most dangerous patch of sand and water in the world, I imagined the coast of Somalia to be a developer's paradise. Every so often, there'd be a wooden fishing boat; and farther out, I could see foreign warships patrolling the shipping lanes. Armed militias, pirates, and hunger had caused the population to flee.

Many Somalis, I would find out later, were starving in refugee camps in Northern Kenya.

The Mogadishu airport runway cuts into the coast, just off the ocean. There are, theoretically, two approaches to the runway: one in from the ocean, and one descending across town and landing toward the ocean. Paul, the pilot, told me that at one point, in better times, it was possible to approach the runway from either end; but antiaircraft rockets coming from rooftops in the city had made the city approach impossible. Now, regardless of the winds, every pilot approached Mogadishu from the ocean, often needing to approach at very high speeds to overcome the headwinds, then slamming on the brakes to stop in time.

Like much of Africa, the Mogadishu airport had a glorious post-independence period. At one point, it offered wealthy Somalis ample flights to exotic global destinations. As would prove to be the case at the other Somali airports we would later travel to, much of the construction of the airports had been done by foreigners. The Soviets had expanded and renovated the airport in the 1970s, before ditching Somalia for Ethiopia. The Americans then picked up the slack and began extending runways and renovating the control tower in the 1980s.

During the Somali civil war in the 1990s, the airport had been completely shut down and flights moved to an airport called K50, about fifty kilometers south of Mogadishu. Now, with increasing security in Mogadishu, the UN and then international commercial contractors moved in to repair and operate the airport. Flying Doctors' flights into Mogadishu had only been possible for about a year, with UN stabilization of the city. Given the unpredictability of jihadist fighting, the flights were frequent but never routine.

As expected, we came in off the ocean and landed fast. The pilots braked aggressively and then taxied to the main terminal. At the tarmac, there were several uniformed security guards, a few soldiers with automatic rifles, and several Filipino UN employees wearing orange reflective vests and holding clipboards. They seemed to be running the operation.

As seems to be the case in many theaters of war, much of the grunt work in Somalia is financed by the West, with work done by a hodgepodge of contractors, soldiers from assorted African countries, and an odd blend of local and expatriate UN workers. Most of the work involved unpacking UN air freighters that were bringing supplies to Somalia—and camouflaged freighters, with cryptic markings, which I suspected were there to replenish weapons and ammunition. The tarmac workers tended to be Asian and were employed by a Dubai-based management company specializing in running logistics in miserable places. Everyone there was making a relative fortune.

Our patients, as would be the case in subsequent weeks, were Burundian and Ugandan troops sent by their respective countries to fight al-Shabaab as part of an African Union commitment (AMISOM, or the African Union Mission in Somalia). AMISOM, which got its start in 2007, was to have been a six-month peace-keeping mission. It would run for nearly sixteen years. It was implemented to stabilize the transitional Somali government that had assumed control of Somalia following the Somali Civil War and to repress the ongoing Islamist resistance. This mission was initially funded by the United States and the European Union in 2007; the US pledged seventy million dollars, and the EU pledged fifteen million euros, to support the mission. So, funded by Western money, troops from Malawi, Nigeria, Burundi, and Uganda were sent to Somalia. Later, troops arrived from Djibouti and Guinea. In that way, Western troops were kept from the front lines, sparing their lives and bad public opinion, while the case could be made that Africans were pursuing their own security interests. It was hands-off and cunning.

In practice, the African soldiers were miserably trained. They wore berets that were all the same color, but uniforms that were different colors. Many shared no common language, and they were housed in horrid conditions far from home. While they were generally successful in reclaiming Mogadishu, the battles with the better-organized Somali militants inevitably led to plenty of avoidable deaths and nasty injuries.

I often wondered what the soldiers thought as they found themselves at war in a dangerous distant country. Young soldiers, no matter where they are from, and at least until they are seasoned, typically convey a sense of inexperience and discomfort with the requirements of their professions. Shooting strangers is probably an alien vocation. But at least when you spend time with Western troops, you feel like there is a sense of moral coherence: this is why we are here, this is what we are doing, and this is why it is good (or at least necessary). There was no such rationalization from the Africans. Most seemed wide-eyed and frightened and utterly unaware of what they were doing in Somalia, other than following orders and collecting a paycheck, as miserable as it probably was.

Once, on a flight, I read about an epidemic of strange illnesses that had popped up among the AMISOM soldiers in Mogadishu, sometime in 2009. Hundreds of young soldiers had become ill with leg swelling and trouble breathing. Dozens of troops had been airlifted with what seemed to be heart failure, and a few had even died from severe symptoms. After the volume of cases of illness had become too much to explain, the World Health Organization launched an investigation. The answer lay in the mess halls and the meager meals of cassava and rice that were provided to the troops. The absence of vegetables and meat had caused the soldiers to become totally deficient in thiamine. As if they were prisoners or refugees, they had developed wet beriberi, something only seen in starvation situations. Investigation done, thiamine was administered to the soldiers, and all symptoms resolved. The situation gave an inkling of how these troops were seen by the UN and by their respective armies.

Once we were on the ground, two paramedics eventually showed up with our three patients. They were ex-British forces medics now working for the British contracting company managing logistics at the airport. I had seen their type before in the Middle East; they were big men, vigilant, and pragmatic. They were part of a cadre of former special forces who left to make money in the private sector and worked in the world's most difficult places. Hardened mercenaries, they were alert and tough and utterly clear about their motivations. These guys would rotate in for a few months, make stacks of money, and then rotate out for a bit. They had no illusions, no false justifications for why they were there. They were not saving the world. This was a transaction. They were not to be messed with.

The three patients that the medics brought were all shy and apprehensive young men—kids, really. They were African soldiers wearing identical light blue cotton pajamas. Two were from Burundi and spoke French; the third was from across the border in Uganda and spoke only Swahili. All three arrived in the back of a converted Land Rover from the clinic in Mogadishu.

The paramedics pulled next to the plane. What I saw when we opened the rear door of the ambulance was pitiable. The soldiers were packed in the ambulance and stank because they were unwashed; their wounds dripped fluids; and their bandages reeked of rot. One soldier lay on a thin cot, while the other two were seated on a fold-out ledge. Flies covered their bloody and infected body parts. The soldier who was lying on the cot was in too much pain to swat them away.

The chaotic heat and the stench were overwhelming, and Lillian and I backed away from the open doors. We took stock of what we had. Our first patient was a teenage Burundian who had been riding on an armored car that had overturned. He had landed hard and was crushed by the car's heavy armor. His chest was smashed. When I opened his pajamas, sections of his chest moved independently as he took breaths. I could see a floating segment of ribs known as a flail chest. He had multiple broken ribs and a collapsed lung, and the doctors in Mogadishu had inserted a tube between his ribs to suck out the blood and air and to re-inflate his lung. Such tubes were typically connected to suction to maintain negative pressure to allow the lungs to expand, but before transferring him, the clinic had tied a string around the end of the tube to secure it, and the plastic stump attached to his chest with hockey tape was filled with dark blood. It looked like a freezer pop.

The second patient was another young Burundian. He had been shot through his leg. It was an AK-47 round, he told me sadly. His lower leg was grossly swollen and firm to the touch. His through-and-through wound had become infected and was dripping pus.

Our third patient, a Ugandan, had multiple shrapnel wounds in his shoulder and back. The shoulder was gangrenous, and there was a foul, watery discharge from his wounds, soaking into thick bandages.

Lillian set to work, establishing new IV lines. Once that was done, she helped get two patients onto flight stretchers. She guided the remaining patient to a seat on the plane. I examined each patient quickly, jotted notes, and then drew up syringes of morphine and administered doses to each soldier.

The first patient—the Burundian with the broken ribs—presented a management challenge. As a first step, I grabbed a pillow from the plane and, using medical tape I secured it to his chest, wrapped long strings of tape around his torso. The pillow would stabilize the flail segment of ribs and would make it easier for him to breathe. His collapsed lung was the next concern. Broken ribs can puncture the lung cavity, leading to a collapsed lung—a pneumothorax. This was probably what had happened to the soldier. We knew that he had at least one pneumothorax, because the doctors in Mogadishu had already placed a chest tube to drain the air between the lung and the chest wall. We'd have to connect the tube to suction in the plane, but the work had been done, at least on that side of his chest.

I ran my hands down the soldier's chest and across his abdomen and back, looking for other wounds. The soldier was young, filthy, and in a lot of pain. He had a decreased oxygen level, but he was breathing well and had otherwise normal vital signs. Under normal circumstances—in, say, a ground ambulance—I would have left well enough alone and transported the patient with oxygen and pain medication. However, transporting a patient with a collapsed lung in an airplane, with different pressure levels, presented an interesting twist. I was suspicious that the soldier had developed a collapsed lung in his opposite lung, as well. I rifled through the files the medics had brought and found the X-ray films the hospital had sent. I held the images up to the sky and, using the sun for illumination, looked for a collapsed lung. I could see the chest tube in on the right chest, which had drained the air and blood appropriately. But on the left side, the opposite side, I could see a small section of collapsed lung, as well. It wasn't big enough to cause problems yet. But we ran the risk that it would get much worse during the flight.

At altitude, due to decreased atmospheric pressure, gases expand. This is one reason why passengers on commercial aircraft often feel bloated after takeoff: gas pockets in the bowel expand in size, causing cramping and flatulence. Even though most aircraft are pressurized, it's only to a pressure corresponding to an altitude of around eight thousand feet. For most people, this is fine; but for someone with a pneumothorax, the pressure changes when moving from sea level to eight thousand feet can cause an insignificant pneumothorax to grow and become a real problem.

Lillian and I had a decision to make. We carried chest tubes and the necessary anesthetic and equipment to put one in, but cutting into a chest wall and inserting a large plastic tube through the rib cage in a fly-infested ambulance on a runway in Somalia is not something one chooses to do easily, especially since the pneumo was small enough that it would likely resolve on its own if we left it alone.

A second option was to wait and see how the patient did at altitude. The problem with this plan, though, was that the pneumothorax, if it expanded, would be on the patient's left side, which would face the aircraft wall in flight. Using a scalpel in a cramped aircraft to surgically insert a tube into a Burundian soldier somewhere above Somalia and the Indian Ocean was also an unattractive option. The fact that I would have to do it from the wrong side of the body—blind, really—was worse.

I looked at Lillian, and then at the Burundian patient, who was slightly more comfortable now that he was receiving morphine. His oxygen levels were holding, if slightly low, and he appeared relatively stable. "Let's go," I said. Time to fly. We'd deal with the smaller pneumo in the air if we had to.

I reconnected the existing chest tube to the plane's onboard suction, and the soldier's tubing quickly filled with a half-liter of dark thick blood. Then it stopped. The soldier coughed a few times and groaned as his lung re-expanded.

The pilots were always delighted to leave Mog. They closed the door, throttled up the engines, and shot toward the ocean, opposite our arrival direction. With the air conditioning and morphine, all three of our patients slept soundly, and the cooler temperatures sedated the flies, which settled on our olive-green equipment bags. For the duration of the flight, Lillian and I stared at the monitor watching the oxygen levels of the soldier with the collapsed lung. Thankfully, they stayed in a safe range.

Michael, who'd spent three hours trying to find a hospital to take our patients, met us at Wilson in Nairobi. The private hospitals in Nairobi were unwilling to take uninsured African soldiers, and the soldiers were ineligible for care at the national Kenyan hospital because they weren't nationals. It was typically hard to find a place to send AMISOM soldiers; it seemed that the African Union was unreliable when it came to paying the bills. It hadn't dawned on me that finding a hospital would be an issue. These were, after all, soldiers who had been seconded to the UN. Maybe naively, I had assumed that the military would take care of things.

Ultimately, Michael located a Catholic charity hospital on the outskirts of town that agreed to care for all three of the men. We loaded them into an ambulance and began a careful ride to the mission hospital in the suburbs of the city. A UN representative met us at the hospital and peered into the van stuffed with the three soldiers.

Lillian and I wheeled the patients into the ED and waited for a sullen, overworked nurse in a starched white cap to take a medical report. There was no oxygen monitor in the ED, and nobody could find a chest tube seal or suction unit—so, as was often the case with the Flying Doctors, our patients were going to get far less monitoring and care than they had received during the flight. This was one of the unfortunate paradoxes of operating an international standard air ambulance in Africa. Lillian said that this type of transfer was nothing new.

We left our three AMISOM soldiers on thin gurneys in the sparsely equipped ED in a city that none had been to before. We gave a quick medical report to the nurse and then to a doctor who passed by, but for the most part, our arrival had been a nonevent for the hospital staff. I was anxious to explain the urgency of surgery for the infection and the details of the pneumothorax. The staff, however, all moved slowly, with purpose but also with a sense of resignation. For their part, our patients, bleeding and infected, watched the scene with only curiosity, no hint of anxiety. We all had different understandings of time and urgency, quality of care, and expected outcomes. Treatment would take place when it took place.

As we walked to the door, I saw our patient with shoulder wounds sitting on a cot in the hall, his new bandages again soaked. He turned to watch us exit, his face expressionless. I had nothing else to say or do. I climbed into the ambulance's passenger seat, and we pulled into the busy Nairobi traffic.

The difficulties and ironies of what we could do and not do washed over me. The security interests of wealthy countries depended on this rag-tag collection of poorly equipped and poorly fed African soldiers. Their access to medical treatment for their horrific war injuries depended on the whims of the administrator of a charity hospital. It felt exploitive. With the plight of those three soldiers weighing heavily on my mind, I took a deep breath. The situation was bigger than all of us. I couldn't change it; no one could. I needed to keep my head turned to the future, to my next patient.

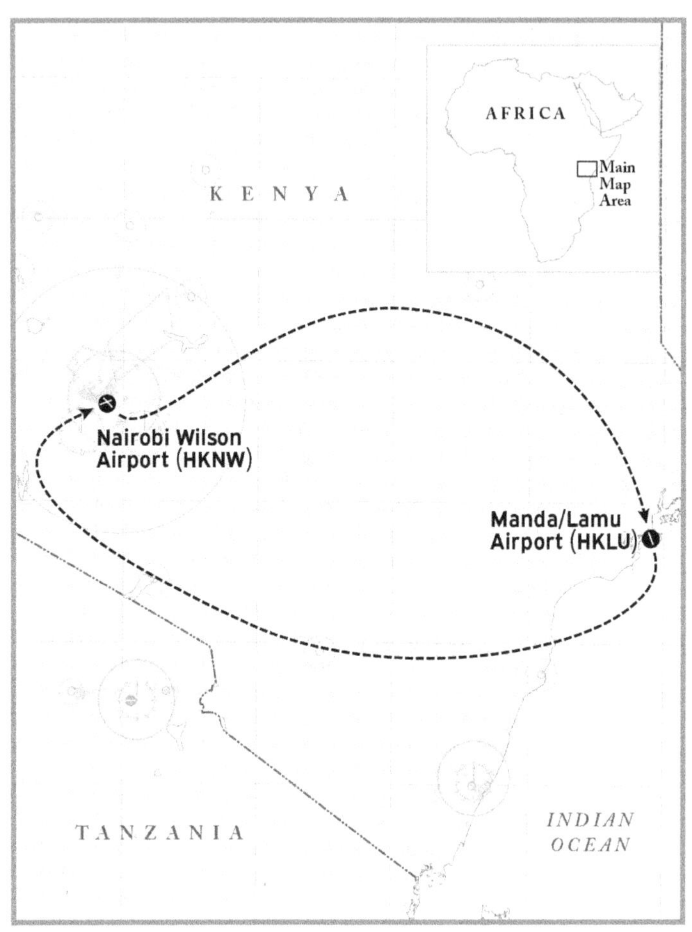

Evacuation from Lamu, Kenya, using a King Air

POINT OF LIGHT

And I believe these are the days of lasers in the jungle
Lasers in the jungle somewhere
Staccato signals of constant information
A loose affiliation of millionaires and billionaires and baby

- Paul Simon

None of us expected to be in the dark, surrounded by American soldiers carrying automatic weapons. But honestly, the entire day had been uncomfortable and strange. This seemed to be a fitting end.

We had left for Manda, an island off the Kenyan coast, at the request of the US embassy in Nairobi. They had called us late in the afternoon requesting an evacuation. It was complicated, though; our patient was a Navy sailor who was still well offshore. The embassy and our administrators and operations folks had gone back and forth on how this would work. He first would be flown by military helicopter to an airstrip on the coast of Kenya, which was adjacent to the small US military camp on Manda Island. We then were supposed to do a handoff at that airstrip and head for Nairobi.

The entire mission was unexpected. The US military's work out of the Manda base was low-profile and secret, mostly special operations. It was deeply unusual that we would get pulled into military work. The American military was highly self-sufficient and had a competent medevac system and decent health care, which was provided at Camp Lemonnier, the big US base located just up the coast in Djibouti. I didn't know how we got involved, but we went where we were needed. I wondered if there was no surgeon at Lemonnier or maybe no transport available. In any case, we were on deck.

The Lamu archipelago on the northern Kenyan coast, which includes Manda Island, is a weird mix of beaches, expensive but bohemian resorts, donkey carts ferrying luxury monogrammed luggage, eco-lodges, therapeutic enemas, yoga retreats, and authentic but charming dhows. A certain type of world explorer hung out there in those days, enjoying the scene, likely oblivious to the fact that American special forces soldiers were stationed right next door at the Manda base and other field camps scattered all along the Kenyan coast. They weren't the only ones; few Westerners understood that there were US troops stationed in East Africa at the time, doing surveillance, special operations, and other dark arts.

The tourists were there to suntan, and the American military was there to hunt and kill pirates and al-Shabaab jihadists—both Kenyan and Somali—who hung out in the region. With the rise of al-Shabaab, there had been an inexorable and palpable slide toward insecurity in the region. But, despite the horrors of the war right across the border, the people around Lamu went about their business as though everything was the same as before, as if nothing had changed. Shops and hotels sold their wares and services to the tourists; the visitors sipped Tusker beer and took photos wearing their linen scarves and muumuus and emailed them to their families in Dusseldorf. But things weren't the same. Islamists from

Somalia floated into Lamu in their rickety boats looking to make money and a name for themselves, and the Americans embedded themselves, playing a long diplomatic and geographic security game while hiding in plain sight.

We set off for the Manda airstrip around seven at night. Our departure was highly unusual, as there are only a handful of lit runways in Kenya, usually only in the cities. Manda had no runway lights, and we would be arriving well after dark. In our flight briefing, the pilots said that the Americans would be arranging for temporary lighting for our landing and takeoff: the details had been coordinated with the embassy attaché.

We left Nairobi headed east, pointed toward the ocean. We approached the coast and could see, to the south, the lights of Mombasa illuminating the horizon. We were headed the other way, north up the coast a few hundred kilometers, toward a dark archipelago. Beyond it: Somalia.

When we got close to Manda, Paul, our pilot, pulled back on the throttle, and we began to descend slowly into the darkness. We could see the lights of the town and lights in scattered homes down the coast; as we got lower toward the airstrip, we saw dense vegetation and nothing else. We were still quite a distance from the town, yet not a single light was visible below. We flew low for a second pass across the peninsula, and we all stared out the windows, looking for some indication that we had arrived. The GPS firmly indicated that we were over the runway.

The US military was supposed to provide temporary runway lighting but, though we were overhead at the arranged time, the airstrip remained pitch black. Paul flipped the plane's radio to an unusual air-to-ground frequency that had been shared with us in advance by the embassy. Suddenly, an American voice came over the radio: we were free to land. The soldiers said they were below and were lighting a flare.

The pilots pressed their faces to the windscreen, and we circled lower looking for the runway light. I wondered for a moment if the military understood that we were a civilian plane with no night vision capabilities. Maybe they were expecting more sophisticated equipment?

Paul pointed the nose out to the ocean, did a big loop, and then came back pointed toward land in the direction the chart indicated the runway could be found. As we got closer, there was a sudden white flash. Soldiers had lit a single strobe light at the threshold to the runway, but nothing else.

Paul was an experienced bush pilot, an African who'd spent his life in Kenya and who'd spent years flying into the African bush doing safari tours before flying for Flying Doctors. He was perhaps the finest pilot I had ever met, and I trusted that he knew when and how to safely take risks. We were all in his hands.

Paul pushed the throttle forward, and the propellers changed pitch and speed. He made a sharp bank right, circling once more, and then lined up our course. I heard the gear drop with a thud and saw the pilots, illuminated by weak red light, run the final checklist and descend into the darkness. Paul leaned forward in his seat and stared out the windshield. He lined up the edge of the window with the strobe light and managed our descent by ensuring that the light didn't sink too far above or below the point he had picked on the window. He approached smoothly, without any last-minute course corrections. The entire descent had been one long uninterrupted arc. Then, we touched down only a handful of feet past the single strobe. The tires screeched once, and the propellers reversed pitch and we decelerated quickly, feeling pressure on our safety belts as we came to an abrupt stop.

We reversed on the strip and, using the landing lights, pulled into a graveled parking area nearby. The pilots killed the engines, and John and I, both covered in sweat from the wild landing, gingerly opened the rear door, peering into near total darkness. Humid air rushed into the cabin, smelling of ocean and sand and plants. A set of headlights from a Humvee illuminated a group of men. I realized that we were surrounded by dozens of US troops, all armed with assault rifles, guarding the plane and the runway and us. A young officer emerged from the shadows, approached the plane, and waited for one of us to emerge.

The baby-faced Lieutenant seemed surprised to see a tall, sweaty American doctor unfold himself through the side door of an African air ambulance. He extended his hand, and I shook it. After he briefed me on the expected timeline, we began chatting about our hometowns and the terrible humidity on the coast. Looking at him in his helmet, full body armor, boots, and rifle, I felt significantly underdressed in my thin white uniform shirt and cotton pants—like I'd misunderstood the dress code.

We were early, and there was time to kill, so we sat on the plane's steps and sipped cold Cokes from our cooler, sharing them with the military corpsmen on the runway. I could see, from the flash of an occasional light, that soldiers had lined the runway and that they could clearly see us in the headlights of the nearby Humvee even though we couldn't see them. I remember feeling quite watched, like an actor on a stage.

The soldiers were all earnest young men. They were apprehensive and watchful and surprised to see me, but also pleased. The group of us ended up huddling in a patch of light, making small talk about military food and the latest sports scores and how one of the soldiers had a foot rash from his wet boots. They were formal and proper, answering in short phrases, each one punctuated by "sir," though of course I was no officer. The young troops' accents revealed that they came from across the United States: Louisiana, Texas, Massachusetts. They were funny, sincere, and modest, each with a certain bravery—a willingness to do the best that they could with what they found when they got wherever they were sent. I realized that we were all there on that remote airstrip through a confluence of world events that had nothing to do with any of us.

It wasn't long before, in the distance and above the noise of the insects, I could hear a heavy thumping. The troops scattered, and they shut off the Humvee lights. A large, dark shadow approached the runway. I remember thinking that I had never seen a helicopter land without flashing strobes or landing lights. The machine was almost invisible; only its massive noise betrayed its presence. Their whole operation functioned with night vision goggles; the environment was kept as dark as possible.

The helicopter landed and shut down with little fanfare. A couple minutes later, two corpsmen dressed in camouflage uniforms and boots walked over to meet us. They carried an envelope of papers and gave me a quick report: it was a young sailor, and they were pretty sure he had appendicitis. They went back to the helicopter and brought the patient, a man in his twenties, to the plane. He was dressed casually in sneakers, a sweatshirt, and track pants. He walked, doubled over, between the medics, while one of them held a partially empty IV bag.

Once he got on the plane, we strapped him in. He was much, much taller than our stretcher; his basketball shoes extended well past the end of the mattress. We checked vitals, and I examined his belly. It was hard and diffusely tender and showed the characteristic signs of peritonitis. I guessed that his appendix had burst and spread infection across his abdomen. Urgent surgery was needed. He'd had antibiotics earlier, so we started another bag of IV fluids and gave him some pain medication. There wasn't much else to do. He needed a surgeon to remove his ruptured appendix and wash out the peritoneal cavity. I wondered how he felt: wherever he had come from— maybe a carrier or a submarine—he had gone, in the span of a few hours, from living in a microcosm of a ship of some sort to the inside of our plane in rural Kenya. It had to be a culture shock. I found myself looking at my young fellow American and feeling a strong paternal instinct, hoping to reassure him that we were a proper organization that did things well, to an international standard, and that he was in good hands.

Getting out of the airstrip would be easier than getting in. So long as Paul lined up correctly with the airstrip's published cardinal direction and accelerated quickly enough, we'd be fine. We dimmed the interior lights, and the Humvee's headlights came on to illuminate the strip. Paul turned on the plane's landing lights and circled back to the runway. With a hand on the throttle, he looked back toward us for a thumbs up. Then he pushed the turbo propellers to maximum thrust, and we accelerated down the dark, bumpy airstrip toward—and then over—the one flashing strobe light the soldiers had placed at the end of the runway. As soon as we were in the air, the single light once again went dark. It had been an extraordinary bit of flying.

Getting a balance of risk versus reward right in any high-stakes rescue work is an art. Air rescues are uncontrolled enough to present a high level of baseline risk, and certain complications—bad weather, bad locations, bad patients—increase the risk. No matter how much routine you put in place, such as running checklists and holding preflight briefings, the unscheduled, non-routine nature of these flights makes them risky. Air medical rescue is among the most dangerous reasons for flying, and helicopters are significantly more dangerous than planes. Helicopter EMS flying doubles the risk of crash fatalities compared to non-EMS helicopter flights; flying at night leads to three times more fatalities; and flying in bad weather, called IFR flying, leads to eight times greater risk.

As a result, air medical services have put in place a range of policies. Progressive ones insist on a second pilot (many helicopters fly with one pilot to save weight and money) and encourage the entire crew to inform the decision on whether to proceed with a flight or not. Many services, for example, don't permit the pilot to know the nature of an emergency before setting off. They want the pilot to evaluate the risks of a flight solely based on weather and other flight variables; they don't want him or her to be influenced by the fact that there is a sick child waiting. Any crew member can refuse any flight unilaterally. If anyone has objections to the flight—feels, say, that the weather is suboptimal, or the mission parameters are too risky—they can cancel a flight, no questions asked.

In Africa, I was always aware that the temptation to push the limits of a flight was exacerbated by Flying Doctor's long history of boldness and dramatic rescues. In many cases, Flying Doctors would be the only service capable of making a rescue in the most remote parts of the continent. If we didn't fly, the patient would die. If we did fly and made the wrong call, we could lose our lives, and the plane, and affect the organization's ability to provide services to hundreds of other patients. This level of personal risk, and the danger of making poor decisions, weighed on all of us.

Sometimes, though, you need to believe in experience and competence. There is no substitute for a pilot or doctor who has thousands of hours of experience. My belief in Paul's abilities never wavered. He was operating at a different level, well inside his zone of competence, this pilot with tens of thousands of hours of flight time in the African bush. Paul had no doubt that he would stick the landing. And neither did I.

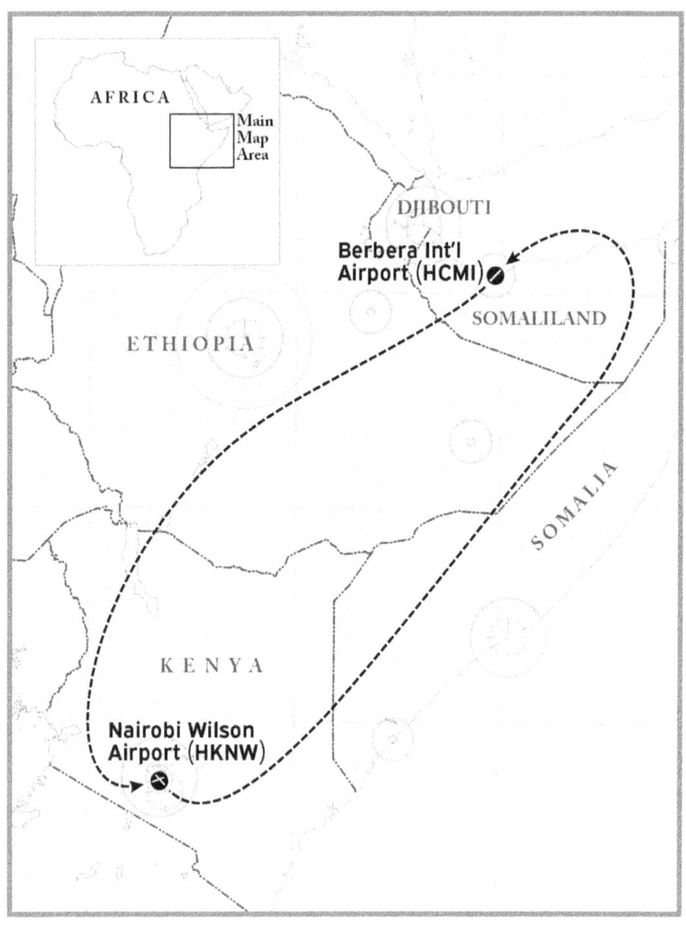

Evacuation from Berbera, Somaliland, using a Citation

PARASITE

Yet may God place a shield of coolest air
Between your body and the assailant sun.
And in a random scorching flame of wind
That parches the painful throat, and sears the flesh,
May God, in His compassion, let you find
The great-boughed tree that will protect and shade

- Sayyid Mohammed 'Abdule Hassan

We flew north, over Kenya, over Ethiopia, Somalia, and Somaliland. For hours, we had soared over an undulating landscape of low, dusty bushes that stretched for hundreds of miles in all directions. Finally, in the distance,

Berbera and the Red Sea came into view. It was an abrupt transition, the pale blue ocean and the uniformly beige land. Outside the windows, the movement and energy of Kenya had gradually slowed into a leisurely but still active Ethiopia, which itself slowed into an empty, tense Somalia, and then into a mostly abandoned Somaliland. From the sky, we watched the continent age from a vibrant youth to something entirely desiccated. Our flight took us over hundreds of kilometers of semi-arid, rocky beige scrubland, broken up only occasionally by settlements and livestock pens.

Somaliland was another African country stuck in geo-political limbo, the legacy of complex tribal and ethnic forces conflated with European colonialism. Somaliland considers itself to be an independent country. But few other international powers agree. Most argue that it remains part of Somalia—though self-managed, in effect, because there had been no functioning Somali central government. Ethnically, most of the population in Somaliland came from one tribe, the Isaaq clan, whose roots in Somaliland go back to the twelfth century; almost all Somalis, including the Isaaq, were Sunni Muslim.

I'd never been in a place that wasn't sure where it

was. But in Somalia and Somaliland, the politics were so vague that one could either be in country "A" or country "B," and the government was so disempowered that it didn't make much difference. For twenty-one-years, people had lived like this. Somaliland wasn't exactly a failed state; it had a small military and seemed to handle the regional affairs and services. But the place wasn't entirely put-together. It was all so tentative.

There was a history to all of this: prior to 1960, Somaliland was a British protectorate. In 1960, it declared independence, calling itself the State of Somaliland, and received messages of support from around the world. Five days later, it voluntarily united with the formerly Italian Somalia to form the Somali Republic. Although unified as a single nation at independence, the south and the north were functionally separate countries—one with an Italian administrative system, and the other with a British one. Mistrust ran deep between the two and, in 1991, Somaliland claimed independence from Somalia—though this time, only Taiwan officially recognized its sovereignty. This ambiguity made it impossible for Somaliland to receive IMF and other development loans and made running a country that much harder. Its GDP was among the lowest in the world. And this is where we were headed: to an airstrip and a town where time stood still.

The Berbera airport was huge and forlorn, eerie, like an abandoned amusement park. It sat on dust. Its runway, at 13,500 feet long, was among the longest runways in Africa, longer even than the runways at the international airports in Cairo or Nairobi. Its length revealed Somaliland's involvement in geopolitics by virtue of its key location on the African horn. Destitute, Somaliland had become enmeshed in Cold War politics right after gaining independence from England. The very long runway had been built by the Russians in the late 1960s to assert themselves and support Soviet expansion in Africa. When the Soviets left in the late 1970s, following the Somali/Ethiopian war, the Americans (as they did in several other African countries) slid in, hoping to counter the Soviet presence in the horn of Africa. The US pumped money into the region by, among other things, renting the airstrip at Berbera at rates which threatened to make it the primary source of national income, ostensibly for use as a backup landing pad for the space shuttle program.

The calculated and transactional nature of the preceding sixty years betrayed Berbera's important historic role as a critical deep-water port. Located at the southern tip of the Ottoman empire, Berbera had long been a bustling trade center, where goods from across Asia—like myrrh, frankincense, coffee, and cinnamon—were traded. The Ottomans were followed by the British, who made Somaliland a protectorate. For a time, Berbera exported shiploads of meat, bound for grills across Arabia and Yemen. So brisk was the business that the Brits referred to Somaliland as "Aden's butcher shop." But by 2012, the ocean traffic and trade had fallen mostly silent. The lack of official recognition of Somaliland, and a lack of consensus around Somalia's governance, made it difficult for aid agencies and international banks to function and provide development loans. Most of the economy ran on remittances sent by Somalis abroad. Though livestock and grains were still produced and exported, the dangerous waters off Somalia had made trade difficult.

The airport at Berbera was mostly abandoned except for UN and international NGO flights and a single commercial flight a day. That flight landed while we were there. It was an old twin-engine passenger plane with no logo on its tail. The passengers boarded quickly while the pilot kept one propeller running; the plane taxied out as soon as people were onboard. Accelerating without stopping, it turned onto the runway, bound for Addis.

Though we were in Somalia, technically, Berbera was safe enough that we needed to take no special precautions. The runway was still in good shape, but there had been no real investment in the airport in decades. Beside the runway sat the exoskeleton of a crashed Russian freighter, long ago stripped for parts, but with the airframe still preserved by the sun and dry winds. Nobody had the time, energy, or money to move it. The terminal buildings were squat white concrete blocks, some decorated with faded Arabic script.

The runway was far longer than we needed, so we touched down and slowly rolled to a stop and then turned in to a massive concrete paved waiting area. The captain shut the engines down, and we opened the door and were hit with an unforgettable blast of heat. It was well over 45 degrees centigrade, and the breeze coming from the interior desert pushed the hot air into the cabin like a convection oven. Sweat rose and immediately evaporated in the heat.

We had arrived in Berbera to collect an Englishman, a young NGO worker who had been working for a feeding program and contracted dysentery. The British have been dealing with dysentery since before they set foot in new lands. King John of England died from dysentery in 1216. So did King Edward in 1302, and King Henry in 1420. Thousands of years later, here we were. Maybe the bugs were winning.

Dysentery is an intestinal infection, caused by contaminated food or water, that causes bloody diarrhea. It's a broad term; a range of pathogens, typically bacteria and parasites, are causes. You typically get it from eating someone's dysenteric expulsions, so it's found in refugee situations and areas with poor sanitation and limited water to wash with.

At the airport, we were initially completely on our own. I decided to poke around an empty concrete and corrugated metal building to find a bathroom. Painted icons guided the way: one was a peeling silhouette of a woman in an abaya. The other was the image of a man in Arabic headdress. We were in an Islamic part of the world. Back at the plane, nurse Mildred, who I was working with for the first time, limbed into a land rover with a ground agent and drove to the front gates of the airport, where our patient was waiting. Thirty minutes later, she returned with James, our patient for the next several hours. He sat in the back seat of the truck, next to his dusty overnight bag.

James was in his thirties, sandy-haired and friendly, with a wide-eyed, idealistic nature. He was in Somaliland as part of a large NGO response to the brewing famine and drought—now a regular occurrence in this hot, arid place.

The living conditions in the NGO camp were rough. A week earlier, James had come down with abdominal pain, severe diarrhea, and fevers. After looking at his stool under a microscope, doctors announced that James had amoebic dysentery, caused by an organism called Entamoeba Histolytica.

Amoebiasis is common in the developing world—there are millions of cases a year. Most cases are uncomfortable but not deadly. The condition is typically limited to bloody diarrhea. But, in a minority of cases, the infection causes a massive inflammation of the colon. Some patients can develop amoebic abscesses throughout the body, which are caused by the amoeba moving through the bloodstream. The danger comes when these amoeba land in places like the liver, brain, and spleen. James contracted dysentery from the microscopic cysts which lived in dirty water in his surroundings, which then developed into amoebic forms in his intestines.

This wasn't a complex case. Normally, the parasitic

amoebas are killed with antibiotics, which James had started and which we continued. His recovery was taking longer than expected, though, which explained the call from the NGO. We started intravenous fluids and got James comfortable, and then we set the air-conditioning to maximum. In Nairobi, he would need two different antibiotics to fight the Entamoeba infection, plus rehydration and correction of his electrolytes, which were out of whack after his intense diarrhea and the terrible heat.

In the meantime, we had another parasite to deal with. Outside in the heat, the captain was negotiating aggressively with a ground handler who had suddenly emerged. From my window, I could see him gesticulating forcefully. At one point, he even walked away from the discussion. The thin Somali ground handler sighed a lot and shook his head every so often. He was handling the pilot with a mix of calm amusement and fake sincerity. The two men were negotiating prices.

It appeared that though the captain had given his best effort, he nevertheless had come out less successful than he had hoped. At one point, clearly near the end of the argument, he turned and headed back to the cockpit and retrieved a stash of US bills wrapped with an elastic band. He took the stack back to the passenger side of the fuel truck, where negotiations were still taking place.

These flights were a hassle. Yes, fuel was hard to import, and the cost of business high. But the officials in Berbera knew there were no better options; once you were on the ground, you had no choice but to pay up. They didn't need to be competitive on price or service, so they weren't. The lack of a proper banking system in Somaliland—the local shilling was not recognized outside Somaliland—made credit card payments impossible. So, the place ran on bags of cash.

In the end, the landing fees at the small, forgotten, ex-Soviet, ex-American airport in northern Somaliland were more than those charged at Heathrow, air ambulance or not. In truth, I never knew how much of the "official fees" and fuel payments we were forced to pay made it back to the airport or fuel company.

Such blatant larceny felt reprehensible. In the absence of an economy, humanitarian evacuations were treated as an opportunity for the locals to make money. It didn't matter that the foreigners were there for purely altruistic reasons. The local bureaucrats didn't care. They were profiteers. As with every other petty corruption, these fees would ultimately be paid by donors and governments, as the cost of doing business.

Despite the corruption, there was a poignancy to the place: this hidden setting was once a thriving town, a hub of intercontinental trade, a cattle and livestock center, a once-self-sustaining entrepreneurial ecosystem. Through circumstances largely outside of its own making, the city and Somaliland itself felt abandoned and left to die. Berbera felt empty, eerie, stuck in-between.

Only parasites remained—the amoebas in the water, and the men who, right or wrong, fed their children by tapping the last remaining economic activity: the help sent by strangers.

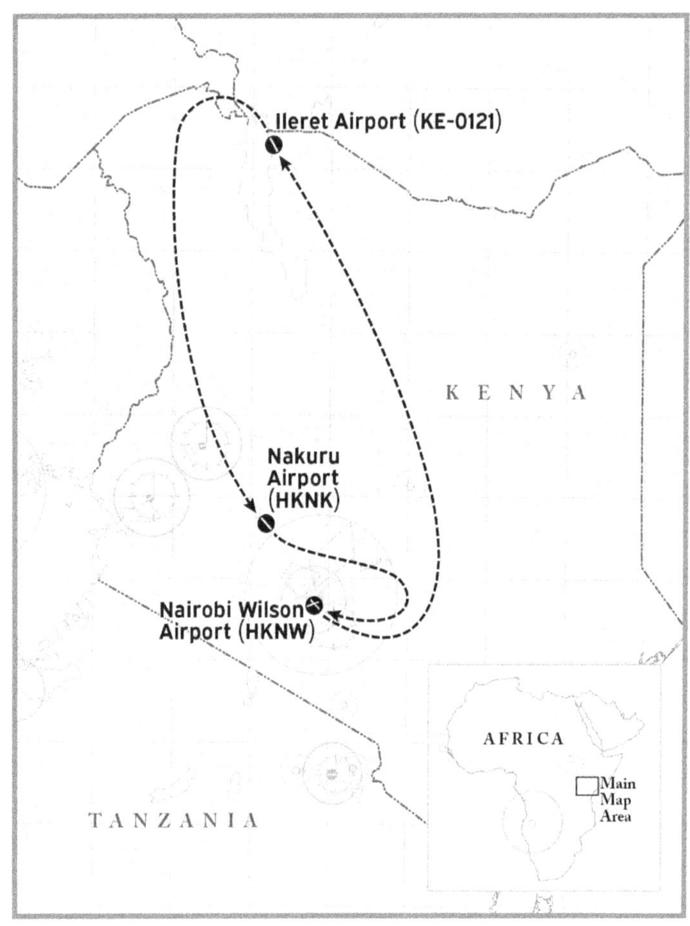

Evacuation from Ileret, Kenya, to Nakuru Kenya, using a Caravan

THIEVES

When the lambs is lost in the mountain, he said. They is cry. Sometime come the mother. Sometime the wolf.

- Cormac McCarthy

His fellow tribesmen lay him on the dirt next to the plane in Ileret, Kenya. He was a skinny fellow, a member of the Daasanach tribe. He wore no shoes and only a traditional pattered wrap around his waist. He'd never been in a car, certainly never in an airplane. Lying under the wing of the plane, shielded from the sun as we worked, he must have been terrified, though I could see no evidence of fear in his face. He was a warrior, assigned to care for the tribe's cattle. He clutched a lone piece of paper on which the nurses at the clinic had inked a medical note in ballpoint pen. We were in Ileret with the Cessna for him because he had been shot by a thief and would otherwise lose his leg.

The Daasanach are a semi-nomadic tribe of farmer/pastoralists who live in the area around Lake Turkana in Northern Kenya, near the Ugandan and Ethiopian borders. You see their homes as you fly through the Rift Valley and into Marsabit County: they are simple igloo-type houses made from branches and covered with hides; wooden walls protect the small courtyards outside the home.

For generations, the Daasanach had lived as their ancestors lived: they grew beans and vegetables and grains when the Omo River was in flood, and they raised goats and cows for milk and meat during the dry season.

In the 2000s, though, the traditional existence of the Daasanach began to grow perilous, and it became much harder to maintain a traditional lifestyle. Part of the reason was the encroachment of modernity. Marsabit County, Kenya, home to the Daasanach tribe, encompasses Lake Turkana, which is a desert lake. Water flows into Lake Turkana from the Omo River in Ethiopia, but the water stays in the lake—no rivers flow out from this lake. As a result, the waters of the lake evaporate, leaving brackish green water which is home to the world's largest collection of Nile crocodiles. The Omo River floods seasonally, and the Daasanach relied on this cycle of flood and retreat to irrigate crops. In 2006, the Ethiopians began construction on the Gibe III hydroelectric dam on the Omo River, which reduced and regulated the flow of the river and stopped the seasonal flooding. At the same time, the Kenyan government leased huge areas of land, used by the Daasanach, to investors who established large-scale commercial farms, mostly to produce export crops.

Yet another challenge was a new level of violence that began to infiltrate Northern Kenya in the 1990s. It wasn't some violent, idealistic Jihad, but pure racketeering—which, in Northern Kenya, meant cattle rustling. On some level, cattle theft has a long history among the African tribes near Turkana. For generations, young men would raid neighboring tribes, and cows would be captured and lost. These raids were an accepted practice; they followed specific rules enforced by elders.

But, by the 1990s, new participants in the cattle rustling business began to appear. With these newcomers, there grew a level of violence that was unknown and something else entirely. Organized criminals, who saw the growing demand for beef in urban areas of Africa, began to steal cattle off the pastoralists' land. In fearless raids, launched in full daylight, they would load cows onto trucks and transport them to abattoirs in urban areas. These raids became increasingly violent as rustlers began to use automatic weapons trafficked from the war zones in the region—especially AK-47s, which could be bought for thirty dollars in the markets. The attacks were coordinated by sophisticated organized crime rings, though the thieves were usually poor young men from other parts of the country who had few other options to make money. For their part, the pastoralists had only rudimentary implements and no experience with modern weapons of war. They were often shot protecting their only source of wealth and status from bandits.

The Ileret airstrip is a small dirt runway adjacent to a tiny, remote village. We had flown hundreds of miles across the African Rift Valley in the Cessna Caravan, landed, and rolled to a stop at the end of the strip. The nurses in the clinic had heard us flying overhead, and one of them soon drove out with the Daasanach teenager in an old land rover. Our young patient spoke neither English nor Swahili, but one of a dozen regional Cushitic languages;

the local nurses did what they could to translate.

The nurses themselves were simple, competent women, locals who had been identified as talented by their schoolteachers and who had ascended their way to nursing college to become some of the most respected people in their village. Every time we interacted with them—whether in the field, like in Ileret, or even in Nairobi—I was taken by their quiet professionalism and intelligence, their careful charting and diligent rounding on their patients. No matter where you ended up on the globe, nursing, like medicine, had its own unique culture: a quiet commitment to patients, at its best never deferential to doctors but respectful and collaborative. These local nurses reminded me why nurses had always been among my favorite people in the hospitals I'd worked in.

Yet, no matter how similar their shared professional identities, there were stark economic differences between African and American nurses—there were such differences among all of us, really. In Africa, I learned, various financial worlds intersected and coexisted. On each Kenyan mission, the physicians, the nurses, and our patients each occupied financial universes that bore no relation to one another— and were often exponential multiples of the others. While I never knew the company financials, I calculated that the King Air burned somewhere around seventy gallons of fuel per hour of flight, and with maintenance and other costs, running costs for the plane were likely in the hundreds or thousands of dollars per hour; while a typical salary for a government nurse in rural Kenya was around $200 per month. The poverty line in rural Kenya, our patient's likely earnings, was $20 per month.

I came to learn that these different, simultaneous economies were a standard feature in poor parts of the world. Such places weren't universally poor; they simply suffered highly dramatic wealth inequality. Every capital city in the developing world had hotels where room rates were essentially Western, and where the housekeeper's daily wage might represent a quarter of a percent of the nightly rate. Places where the elites drove Porches and hired poorly paid guards to protect their cars from the child beggars who went from table to table at the café restaurants in fashionable parts of town begging for french fries from the patrons.

That was the funny thing about medicine, at least how we were practicing it: our work meant that these discrete economic systems intersected. At least for a few moments, on missions like these, we each occupied a common world, shared stories, and came to recognize our common humanity.

When we arrived in Ileret, John and I sat on the ground next to our patient, whom I examined head to toe to make sure that we hadn't missed another injury. The damage seemed limited to his right leg, where the clinic nurses had applied small gauze pads to two wounds. I removed the gauze and saw that the wounds were oozing foul discharge. The boy's entire leg was tense, and from the location of the wounds, I could tell that his bones were likely shattered. The AK-47 shoots an enormously powerful cartridge—it's a military bullet designed to tumble through tissue so as to create the most damage; it leaves a cone-shaped path of destruction bigger than the size of the bullet itself. I felt for a pulse in the patient's foot. It was there, but weak, and his foot was cool.

Given the firmness of the leg, I suspected compartment syndrome. Compartment syndrome can occur in many parts of the body, but legs and arms are well-known sites. Legs are separated into "compartments" by sheets of fascia. In the thigh, there are two compartments; in the lower leg, there are four. After trauma, swelling and pressure can build up in one or more compartments, and this pressure can impede blood circulation, making the loss of a limb a real possibility.

Compartment syndrome is diagnosed by inserting a needle manometer into the different compartments. The pressure in these spaces is normally low, but it can rise to high levels after an injury. The treatment for compartment syndrome is primitive but effective: surgeons must perform what's called a fasciotomy, where they open the sheets of fascia and create space for the swelling. The pressure is thus relieved, and blood circulation resumes. In my estimation, this was an injury that needed just such urgent orthopedic surgery, or the loss of our patient's limb was guaranteed.

We wrapped the boy in a yellow tarp, and, trying to support his broken leg, we loaded him in the Caravan. I sat next to him but had nothing to say. He smelled of earth and sweat and livestock and infection. Wounds in this part of the world became easily infected in the tropical heat. John started an IV in the boy's hand, and we started antibiotics and gave him a shot of morphine for what was certainly severe pain. We had no way to gain his consent. We did what was best, and the boy willingly and trustingly accepted our help. Our Daasanach warrior accepted his first plane ride with stoic resolve and great courage. As the engine turned over and our strobes and landing lights came on, he stared at the ceiling and didn't move an inch.

The operations crew worked hard to find an accepting hospital for all our patients. On this run, they found a Christian charity hospital, only a forty-five-minute flight away, that had an orthopedic surgeon available and was willing to treat our patient. There was an airfield next to the hospital.

On the landing, the pilots overflew the hospital field a few times. It couldn't be called a runway: it was a simple strip of dirt and grass, surrounded by acacia trees on both sides. But it was big enough for the Cessna. Someone at the hospital had been helpful and lit an outdoor fire in a barrel. The thick smoke drifted and let the pilots gauge the crosswinds.

We touched down and stopped at the end of the field, near the hospital's boundary wall. The hospital was a simple, single-story building with a garden and a tin roof. I could see someone open the gate to the field and motion in the distance.

The village's children had heard us coming. As soon as we landed, a group of thirty local school kids ran to the plane and stood at a respectful distance, watching as we opened the doors and prepared to transfer the warrior. They were different ages, some in proper school uniforms—green skirts and sweaters—and carrying bookbags. Others were dressed in T-shirts and printed skirts. The smallest children stood on plastic water jugs for a better view. None wore shoes. They craned their necks to see what was happening.

A few minutes later, two nurses wearing impeccable formal white nursing dresses and caps, and two doctors in starched white coats, emerged from the gate. They pushed a thin metal gurney with tiny wheels on it that clattered across the field. The gurney seemed dainty, a pipe-framed model from 1950, but it was in good shape. We lifted the warrior onto it and covered him with the crisp sheet they had brought. We then signed a clip-board full of forms and watched as the nurses pushed the gurney across the field to the hospital. The children remained fascinated by the plane. We were the event of the week. By now, the field had become the village center. Some children rolled inflated inner tubes with sticks; others, carrying heavy jugs of water hauled up from the river, stopped to stare at the plane and wave. These were lovely kids—well cared for, curious and unspoiled, and wearing enormous smiles.

We packed up, closed the doors of the Caravan, and got onboard. The copilot shouted a warning from his window, and the kids all ran to the edge of the field. The pilots stared intently down the field and were satisfied that there were no children or goats on our path. With a great cloud of noise and dust, we bounced down the field and lifted off.

From the air, I looked back at the boy being wheeled into the hospital building. He had no family with him, no possessions or phone or money. He was brave, but he had been no match for modern evils. The old ways wouldn't work much longer.

I hoped someone would look out for him.

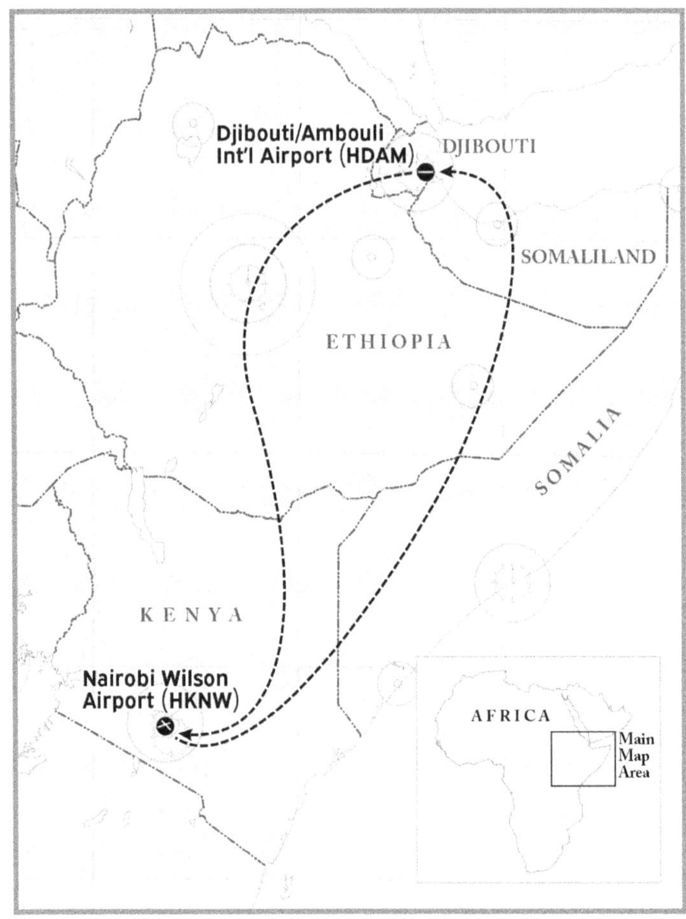

Evacuation from Djibouti using a Citation

DEADLY PERSISTENCE

The air is full of the laughter of machines,
The metallic joy, fresh, as if seas had suddenly
Flooded the land and purged away despair.

— Margaret Stanley-Wrench

Military bases were Djibouti's claim to fame; the tiny nation located on the east coast of Africa, just above the Horn, didn't have much else to sell. Besides the French, who had a base in Djibouti, and from whom Djibouti had claimed independence in 1977, the Americans, Italians, Chinese, and Japanese had all built their own bases in the neighborhood. Each was there due to Djibouti's geostrategic importance—it sat at the mouth of the Red Sea down the coast from the Suez Canal. It was central to the world's busiest shipping lanes. Many countries wanted a piece of the coastal real estate, and others wanted to be close (though not too close) to the sources of Islamic terrorism on the Horn of Africa—Yemen was across the narrow channel of water, the Ban al-Mandab Strait; Somalia was due south. In any case, the bases were a growth industry for a poor but well-located and somewhat indiscriminate country without a lot of other options for making money.

Camp Lemonnier in Djibouti was a once-obscure airbase that grew in scale and importance to the Americans after Somalia became an international toothache. It had, at one point, been a French Foreign Legion base named after a French army general, Emile Rene Lemonnier. The Americans moved in around 2002. Apparently, after years of misspelling Lemonnier's name, they grudgingly added the second *n*. The base is a big place, 600 acres. Given its location, it became central to US military anti-terrorism efforts in the Middle East and Africa. Night and day, military jets left for patrols as far away as the Arabian Gulf. The base shared space with the international civilian airport. One side featured military hangars and military barracks, while the other featured an international terminal that was used for regular flights across the region and into Europe.

We were headed to the domestic side of the airport to collect a sick military contractor. He was one of thousands of employees who worked for the contractor that built and maintained the American base, fed the soldiers, and cut the grass. It turned out that this outsourcing of base management was a common phenomenon: Kellogg Brown & Root, now known as KBR, is a Houston-based, publicly traded company that specializes in exactly this work. The firm collects huge contracts from the US military to build and operate military bases and embassies around the world. They specialize in building impenetrable facilities in tough places, fast. These sorts of companies collect huge fees and hire people from around the world to do the day-to-day tasks of running a base—cooking, cleaning and facilities management, waste, power, vehicle maintenance, driving, security, and so on. The outsourced contractors provide labor at lower costs than the military can, and their salaries don't include military benefits.

Such massive defense contractors made me deeply uneasy. Despite all the money apparently flowing into these few square miles, as we descended, all I could see outside the immediate walls of the airport were tin roof shanties and dirt roads. Of course, KBR and the US military's goal in running a base in Djibouti was patently not to redistribute wealth, but to serve themselves. Achieving this meant there were multiple simultaneous economies in play at this interface between the West and the rest of the world.

In 2012, KBR's annual revenue was over eight billion dollars, six times higher than that of Djibouti's entire gross domestic product. In Djibouti, money flowed like a roaring river: a huge current at the beginning, with funds diverted all along the river's course, ending in a trickle of mud. The money often came from Western governments, and all the biggest beneficiaries were well upstream: the Western lobbyists, consultants, and contractors who provided materiel and support and bribes. When, finally, these rivers crossed into the developing world, they were reduced to a pittance. The locals, if they were fortunate enough to hold jobs, drew their water from these trickles with thimbles.

I was skeptical that business at this scale, in these sorts of places, could be done in above-board ways; funneling that kind of money through a poor country had to encourage bad behaviors. Indeed, it didn't take long to find that a few months earlier, in Spring 2012, the former CEO of KBR had been sentenced to prison for participating in a decade-long scheme to bribe Nigerian government officials to obtain contracts. Upon sentencing, he ruefully claimed that his decision to bribe officials had been fueled by "ambition, ego, and alcohol." So it went.

We were glad to land in Djibouti uneventfully. The pilots said that the local air traffic controllers were known to be overworked; and the recent addition of a fleet of unmanned drones, also needing to land and take off, had only made the approach and landing that much more challenging. The Americans, not long before, had made Djibouti their main base for drone flights covering East Africa and Yemen. Another base was in the works for West Africa, which also had developed a militant Islamic problem. The drones needed to take off and land, but obviously landing via remote control was harder than landing with full sensory perception. Mixing drones into the landing sequences took significant concentration on the part of the local Djiboutian controllers.

Nevertheless, we did land safely. We pulled off the runway and taxied past the military field. Medically, this was to be an uneventful, even routine, call: a Pakistani civilian contractor had developed chest pain the night before. We had been asked to bring him to Nairobi for a cardiac catheterization. There wouldn't be much for us to do: EKG, make sure aspirin had been given, manage pain, and watch for cardiac dysrhythmias.

Across the tarmac, as we pulled in, I could see an extraordinarily long row of drones parked near a hangar. They were bigger then they'd appeared in the pictures. They were the size of vans, and in person they looked lethal and otherworldly—a pack of smooth, oblong killers. Their appearance was jarring; I realized that the windshields of planes are somehow comforting. They make us feel as though the plane has "eyes," or at least that there are humans behind the glass who do. But the Reapers, the drones that were lined up on the military side of the airport, have a smooth, aerodynamic, windowless forepart. They resemble nothing so much as blind metallic aliens sent to exterminate us. I looked at them with the fascination and fear I'd have for an exotic viper.

The Reapers, as the name suggests, were designed to harvest people. They had just entered service in 2008 when I first arrived in Africa and were the result of a military competition. The US Air Force had wanted a more powerful drone than the starter-set drones they owned. So, they opened a competition to see who could build a class of "hunter-killer" drones that could fly high and for a long time.

The Air Force ended up selecting the Reaper, which had engines that were almost ten times as powerful as their original drones, with the ability to cruise faster and hold more bombs than ever. Their other big advantage was their ability to stay put for hours, flying in circles, watching and waiting. This ability was called *deadly persistence* by the military; the drones were so quiet that you'd have no idea they were miles above you. Their cameras could pick up the smallest details; their bombs could land in a teacup. I read that there were three hundred drones across Africa. Each one cost thirty million dollars. Across from us, parked along the runway, were ten billion dollars in hardware just sitting there. It was a breathtaking realization.

Our captain pointed to the Reapers and told me with a laugh that the drone pilots were sitting in dark rooms near Las Vegas. They came to work, punched in, then maneuvered the Reapers via satellite, surveilling Yemen and Somalia from fifty thousand feet. Almost ten miles up. When the time was right, the "pilots" could push a trigger on their consoles and release the bombs. Then, at the end of the day, presumably after they stopped by the lunchroom to reheat their leftovers and get coffee, the pilots punched out and went home to their suburban bungalows and lawns and casino happy hours. It was a hard, almost surreal thing to consider. Our own flights in Africa, in contrast, were visceral and real. We got dirty and slick with sweat, and we felt every bump of the turbulent air and every divot in the runway. The drone pilots were never fully here. They kept both feet in Vegas, interacting entirely virtually over a TV screen. If our plane ran into a Reaper on final approach to the runway, we would be killed while the Reaper pilot clearly would not. Being present made us far more invested in monitoring our environment, being part of the ecosystem, taking thoughtful risks, and sharing the skies.

With the ambulance delayed at the airport, I stared across the tarmac while a Reaper was being fueled. I'd run into the American military several times on our recent journeys across East Africa and still hadn't reconciled my feelings about their presence. What were my countrymen doing in Africa? Was this how our government funds should be spent? Did citizens in the US know that they—we—had paid billions for drones and facility management contractors on the Horn of Africa?

Or that the Americans were in East Africa, at all? Or why? The daily goings on of the US military—even those that weren't official secrets—were opaque to the average citizen. It seemed that only when something went wrong, when there was a digestible story for average people to latch onto, did US citizens understand the depth of American military involvement across the world.

That opacity concerned me. I was extraordinarily proud of America during its best moments—those times when it stood for democracy and freedom and decency. There was no other country like it.

One afternoon, maybe a year before my trip to Africa, I stood at a naturalization ceremony with other immigrants. Our ceremony was on a hot day, and I was surrounded by teary families in their Sunday best, all of us holding small American flags as we recited the oath of allegiance to the United States. We promised to support the Constitution and to defend the United States against its enemies. Then, a judge proclaimed us Americans. It had taken two decades for me to become a naturalized citizen; it was something that had been important to me. I wanted to engage with, and participate in, American democracy and give back to this extraordinary country that had welcomed me, supported my aspirations, and trained me as a doctor.

But my deep patriotism didn't and couldn't conceal my lack of confidence in US military decision-making—or my concerns about the terrible power and misaligned incentives of the American military-industrial complex. In my pledge to the country as a new citizen, I swore "faith and allegiance" to the United States, but this pledge didn't require me to approach our nation's collective actions with a dispassionate eye or even blind obedience. My skepticism, like many Americans', was born after 9/11 as we witnessed our country nurse its wounds by plotting a series of terrible military misadventures—in Libya, in Afghanistan, and (most especially) in Iraq. We knew that, after years of bloodshed and the overthrow of Saddam Hussein, the 9/11 Commission was ultimately unable to verify that there had been any weapons of mass destruction in Iraq; nor did Iraq have any links to Al Qaeda. The terrible loss of lives suffered during our invasion and occupation of Iraq was made worse by the fact that we'd had no reason to be there at all.

Everybody thinks they are an expert after watching the evening news, and I was conscious of the fact that I had no particular knowledge of Iraq. I wasn't a war analyst by anyone's criteria. But America's big footprints in East Africa—the way we took over bases and issued massive contracts and RFPs and arranged for partnerships of convenience to further geopolitical aims around the world, while dropping bombs from remote-controlled Reapers—left me troubled. I wished I had more confidence in these decisions. History proved, again and again, that flawed American military engagements were more easily entered than exited.

To be clear, I was no Pollyanna. The US military's work was necessarily ugly and was an unavoidable use of federal monies. It was also obvious that Somalia had become a nidus for Jihadist terrorism; piracy on the Red Sea was a global supply chain concern; the Middle East was a tinderbox; terrorism was on the rise in the Sahel—Mali, Burkina Faso, Niger—and North Africa was a mess. It was a sad fact that, left unchecked, instability would spread across borders with global consequences. In Kenya, in 2011 and 2012, there had been a dozen attacks by al-Shabaab terrorists that killed dozens and injured hundreds of people. The Islamists attacked police stations, nightclubs, bars, churches, shops, and a bus station; their victims were just ordinary people going about their daily lives.

Hiding from these problems was not an option.

The world was getting more and more intertwined and global. I thought of *The New York Times* columnist Tom Friedman's frequent articles on what he called the age of acceleration. He described the tricky confluence of rapidly improving technology, increasing globalism, and climate change. These three factors were changing the world more quickly than existing economic, political, and social systems could keep up with. The resulting turmoil—unemployment, disaffection, refugees, and hunger—meant that there would be no foreseeable end to these heroic interventions, including in Africa. Globalism would make regional problems global ones far more quickly than in years past—which is why bases had become a boom business in Djibouti.

On the tarmac, we were all loaded up. John got a stack of papers from the base military team, and we strapped in our Pakistani patient for the ride back to Wilson. He was stable, and I elevated the head of the stretcher so that he could look out the window. As we went by, he pointed out the window at a dirt lot and said that the engineers and construction workers were on their way to bulldoze another section of scrub adjacent to the field. There were plans to dramatically expand the base to make room for more people and drones; they were outgrowing the existing base facilities.

Who knew if it was the right call? We all—Americans and Africans, alike—needed to have confidence that this growth, these massive investments and the consequent spilled blood, were carefully considered and intelligently done. I crossed my fingers and hoped that our leaders would live up to their responsibilities. It was an open question.

I was sure, though, that KBR would do just fine. The investments had been promised, the tax dollars appropriated, the contractors' contracts signed, the drones fueled, and the quarterly earnings reports prepared. There was too much momentum for the base boom to stop, and investments in the "war on terror" would only go up over time as global entropy increased. Looking out the window, I considered, for a nanosecond, logging onto my online broker to purchase some KBR stock. I had no doubt that it would turn out to be a wildly lucrative long-term investment. A home run.

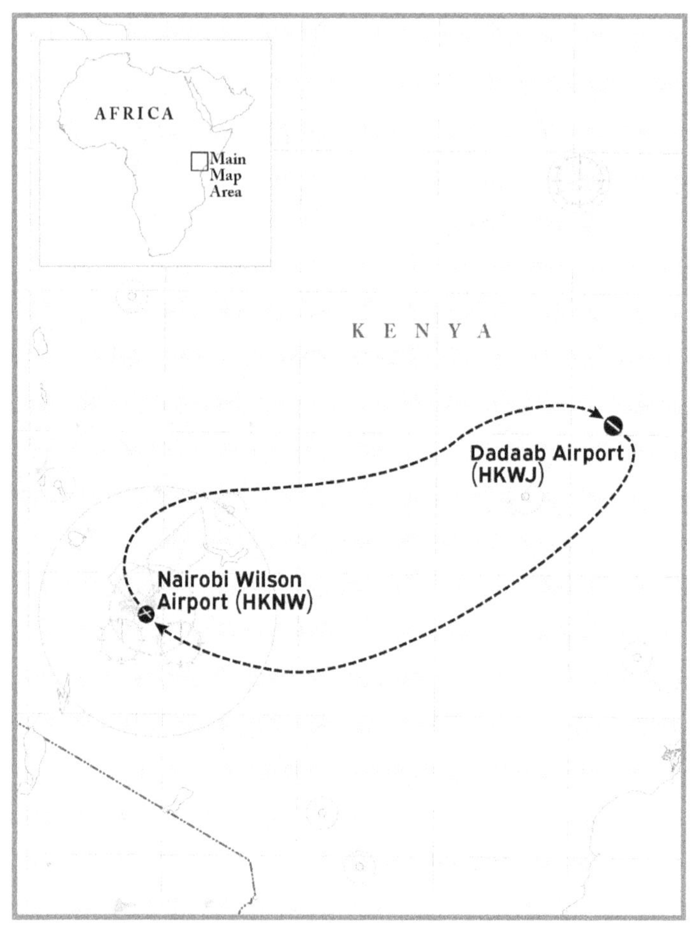

Evacuation from Dadaab, Kenya, using a King Air

MUSELMÄNNER

Schwarze Milch der Frühe wir trinken sie
abends
wir trinken sie mittags und morgens wir
trinken sie nachts
wir trinken und trinken

Black milk of morning we drink you evenings
we drink you at noon and mornings we drink
you at night
we drink and we drink

- Paul Celan

In northeast Kenya, about a two-hour flight north of Nairobi, the beige, barren plains of the border between Kenya and Somalia are interrupted by an almost endless sprawl of white plastic tarps flapping in the wind. These tarps made the roofs and walls of the primitive shanties of the refugee camp called Dadaab. The shanties stretch for miles—there are tens of thousands of them—and extend beyond the camp's centrally-positioned airstrip. A small trading town in the predominantly Muslim area of northern Kenya has, over the past twenty years, become the largest refugee camp in the world. In 2012, Dadaab held nearly half a million Somali refugees in an area originally designed to hold ninety thousand.

With its dwellings made of sheets of plastic and the branches of the local scrub bushes, Dadaab, from the air, most closely resembled an enormous garbage dump. Sometimes, there were domed tents; and every so often, there was an official building—a school, a feeding station, a health clinic—structures that were sturdier than all those that surrounded them. But the rest of the dwellings were primitive, cobbled together lean-to shanties. By 2012, Dadaab had been in existence for twenty-one years, created in 1991 to house the refugees fleeing from the civil war in Somalia. To have improved the facilities too much would mean admitting that Dadaab was there to stay, which was probably true—and probably intolerable to Kenyans, who had initially consented to the camp's creation with the understanding that it was a temporary accommodation in the face of short-term upheaval. Various NGOs ran the place—different ones for different sectors of the camp: the Norwegians in one area; the British in another; the Germans in yet another.

Dadaab routinely experienced crises: floods, outbreaks of cholera, the kidnappings of aid workers, shootings, and the explosions of improvised explosive devices. Despite these tragedies, the air freighters kept coming. They were filled with donated bags of grain and cooking oil and refeeding paste, all arriving in burlap bags or boxes stamped with the UN logo or that of some other benevolent Western nation.

Most of the refugees in the camp had walked hundreds of kilometers across the Somali border into Kenya. They were escaping violence, jihadists, civil war, and—more recently—the famine caused by severe drought. As improvised as it seemed, there was nothing fleeting about the camps that made up Dadaab. An entire generation had been born there, some of its residents children who had never known another life. These were people living in a holding pattern, lacking papers, identities, and nationalities. They weren't wanted in Kenya and weren't safe at home…or what was left of it.

In Dadaab, there was no stable community, there was no economy, no mercantile, no growth. It was a holding pen. I had never seen anything that had less sense of possibility, of movement. Some refugees had been there for so long that they had the listless energy of convicts on death row. There were no prison walls, but escape was impossible; there was nowhere to go.

Kenya kept threatening to close the camp, convinced that—with its 97 percent Somali Muslim population—it had become a recruiting center for al-Shabaab. But even as the situation in Somalia improved, given the camp's massive size, closing it and expelling hundreds of thousands of refugees to the streets would be an impossible logistics challenge which the Kenyans weren't able to handle. So, Dadaab stayed open, a victim of its own inertia, which was a bad side effect of terrorism and failed government policies made thousands of miles away.

The Dadaab airstrip itself sat close to the center of the camp. It was surrounded by a professional chain-link fence with rows of barbed wire strung across the top. Private security, mostly contractors, patrolled the perimeter of the landing strip. These were men in trucks, holding machine guns. The gate to the airstrip looked like the entrance to a military base, with guards posted out front. Any wood or organic groundcover which had existed on this barren plain had long ago been chopped up and burned for fuel. As such, the persistent wind which blows across the northern Kenyan plains whipped up infinite brown clouds of dust that swirled around the dwellings and covered the runway. It gusted dramatically as we landed, covering everything nearby.

Like our recent flights to Somalia, trips to Dadaab had become a habit. Every few days, we would be sent to its dusty airstrip to collect sick UN employees and aid workers. On this flight, we had left Wilson early. It was our third flight to the camp that week. We knew the routine. We would leave Nairobi, the urban area fading to a green tapestry of small farms and villages before abruptly becoming flat, brown, and featureless. Then, after a two-hour flight, we would circle the flimsy dwellings of the camps and touch down in the dust. We would be met by "security"—groups of young men holding AK-47 rifles, wearing pants barely secured by thick leather belts and falling off their skinny frames, ill-fitting sweaters that hung in the neck and off their arms, and plastic flipflops. This day, the young men languished under a tree and watched as the United Nations ambulance passed the gates and approached the plane.

The inept security worried the captain, who was always in a rush—"Make it a load-and-go," he'd say. There had been recent bomb attacks in Dadaab directed at Kenyan police officers and aid workers. A few months earlier, two Spanish aid workers, with the aid group Doctors Without Borders, had been kidnapped by Somali militants in the camp and were still being held hostage. Around the same time, kidnappers had ambushed multiple vehicles by the camp, shot several workers, and had taken and held four Norwegian Refugee Council employees hostage for four days, before a rescue mission was launched. As a result of all the violence, the NGOs were beginning to pull out of Dadaab. It was a highly risky place and time.

Apart from that, it was business as usual. The UN ambulance met us on the tarmac. We found our patient in the back, fast asleep and snoring. This time, he was a young man in his twenties, well-built and strong, a Kenyan. His hands were tied to the stretcher, at the wrist, with muslin triangle bandages. I read the notes quickly: Gacoki had been working for the UN for a few months in the camp. His coworkers had watched his mood deteriorate, and he had become more tired and depressed and withdrawn. One evening, friends had found him in his quarters, hallucinating, hearing voices, and acting aggressively. At the clinic, doctors had diagnosed him as suffering from a depressive psychosis.

According to the nurse who escorted him to the runway, when the doctors had told him of their plans to send him to Nairobi, Gacoki had jumped off the stretcher in the UN infirmary, smashed through the front door, and run from the facility, disappearing through the passages between the shanty tents. The security guards, uncharacteristically, had mobilized and chased and tackled him before dragging him back to the clinic. There, he screamed out loud, unintelligible words. They were the cries of a man hearing voices, mixed with the legitimate fears of flying, of doctors, and of losing his paycheck if he had to leave. The doctors knocked him out with a strong sedative, tied him to the stretcher, and then drove him to the airstrip in the back of a UN ambulance—all entirely against his will. There was nothing else to do. And so, we took him into our care.

On those frequent trips to Dadaab, the children always stood out to me; the older kids would always show up for our arrival, grouping together by the dozens. They'd stare through the fence, fixated on our aircraft, their fingers reaching through and clenching the chain-link. We would also hear the younger ones, the babies, in the tents beyond the runway. Their endless wails became the camp soundtrack to me.

The intense attention from the children demanded self-reflection. I saw myself clearly through their eyes—a novelty, a welcome distraction for sure. But the kids understood our comings and goings and probably knew that I, unlike them, was free to come and go as I pleased. Sometimes, they saw me leaving and re-arriving two or three times a week. I had a degree of mobility, of freedom and empowerment, that they would never enjoy. I don't think that they envied me. I think that the yawning expanse between our options and opportunities made my life an unimaginable existence. Our show was watched with enthusiasm, but it was nothing the children would imagine they could emulate or aspire to. Wrapped in my mantle of privilege, the greatest of which was a future, I saw Dadaab for what it was, a hellish home to hundreds of thousands of otherwise homeless beings.

Truthfully, my status was uncomfortable. I wanted to get in and get out. The Dadaab flights, arriving at the camp in an expensive aircraft, made me deeply self-conscious; just being in the camps brought forth an anger within me—but also despair, shame, and guilt.

My feelings stemmed, I thought, from a feeling of impotence combined with a desire to help and a shame for what I had and what I took for granted in my life. Our crew of four felt powerless in the face of such horrors. We were unsure of how to respond to misery on such a large scale. I tried, without much success, to justify our presence by arguing that we were saving lives—but, of course, there were perhaps tens of thousands of lives in Dadaab being lost in the camp at any point. Those were the deaths for which we hadn't and wouldn't be called.

When I was a high-school student, I studied the American liberation of Dachau, the infamous German concentration camp complex. I recalled a terrible story (one of an almost endless many): the first US troops, when they entered the camp in 1945, were stunned by the thousands of walking, hollowed-out skeletons who greeted them. The weakest—the most emaciated and listless of these people, existing somewhere between life and death—were known by the prisoners as "Muselmänner." It's an odd word that refers to those prisoners who were exhausted and dying of starvation, who seemed resigned to their deaths.

The American troops, hoping to help in any way

in the face of such shocking suffering, reflexively gave the starving Muselmänner chocolates and other rich foods from their rations. Within hours, many of those inmates who had received the chocolates and food had died from refeeding syndrome. Their emaciated bodies had inadvertently been given too many calories, too quickly, and the subsequent rapid shifts in their electrolytes caused by the metabolism of the dense food had killed them. Eventually, the military sent in medical teams and engineers to manage the supply of food and water to the malnourished victims.

It was such a sad story of people with the best of intentions trying to help in the only way they knew how, amid calamity at a super-human scale. It may have medically been the wrong thing to do, but I deeply understood the instinct to help in any way possible. Like those soldiers in Dachau, I also felt a strong human instinct to intervene and try to alleviate the suffering which suffused the camps at Dadaab.

At the same time, I was ashamed that I couldn't wait to be gone from that place. I was ashamed, even, of helping the sick UN aid worker who was our patient. Because my contribution was nothing. A grain of sand on a beach.

I stood outside the plane and looked around at the guards and burning garbage and refugees eking out lives in this liminal place. We had all become captives of the jihadists. Their poisoned ideas and the threat they presented held the region hostage— indeed, held the whole world hostage. Countries were spending trillions of dollars to fight these jihadists, whose impact far outstripped other threats. But for the people of Dadaab, the world had done nothing but leave them to die in squalor.

Somalia and its problems had been created by forces far bigger than us. Fixing those problems was not something we could do. For every life we saved, there were thousands adjacent that we didn't. Planes were called for staff, not refugees.

Gacoki's sedative wore off as we were lifting him into the plane. His eyes wandered around the cabin. He looked at us curiously, but without fear and without mania. I had a large syringe of sedative drawn up in my breast pocket, and I was prepared to give him a big dose if he made any trouble. But he made none. On some level, Gacoki knew that it was time to go. He turned on his side and closed his eyes and left Dadaab far behind.

Often in the evenings at the Aero Club in Nairobi, when I had time after flights, I would read Dr. Tom

Reese's memoir describing the founding of the Flying Doctors— and, later, Dr. Anne Spoerry's memoir, *They Call Me Mama Daktari*. Both books told extraordinary stories of altruism. The doctors flew their Cessnas to the savannas to fix ordinary people. Their adversaries were largely microbes and wounds and human pathology.

In contrast, in 2012, our adversaries were broken humans, the consequences of failed ideologies, Cold War geopolitics, Islamist uprisings, the hapless UN, and the ever-expanding military-industrial complex. The issues that created the patients we now served were far harder to fix. They required more than an idealistic doctor in an airplane.

As we flew toward Nairobi, I wondered whether there was a danger in becoming sentimental about the archetypal story of the visiting missionary doctor and the grateful African tribesman patient. Africa had long been a scene of conflict. In the twentieth century, global ideologies and Cold War tensions had played out in proxy fights across the continent, lasting for decades. African governments were unstable, coups were regular, and periodic theocratic uprisings were not uncommon.

There would have been nothing admirable about Flying Doctors standing back from the geopolitics and conflict and pain of the new era. We had no choice but to engage with the wars and refugee camps and violence in East Africa. Faced with such atrocities, most of us instinctively want to become the best humans we can be, even if we are overwhelmed by the scale of what faces us. I, too, felt a professional obligation to help. But for now, I could only stare at the piles of garbage-bag housing and pluck out the occasional, lucky soul. One starfish, among a holocaust of dying sea life, raised its arm, begging to be saved from the mud.

Along the strip of wet sand that marks the ebbing and flowing of the tide, death walks hugely and in many forms...

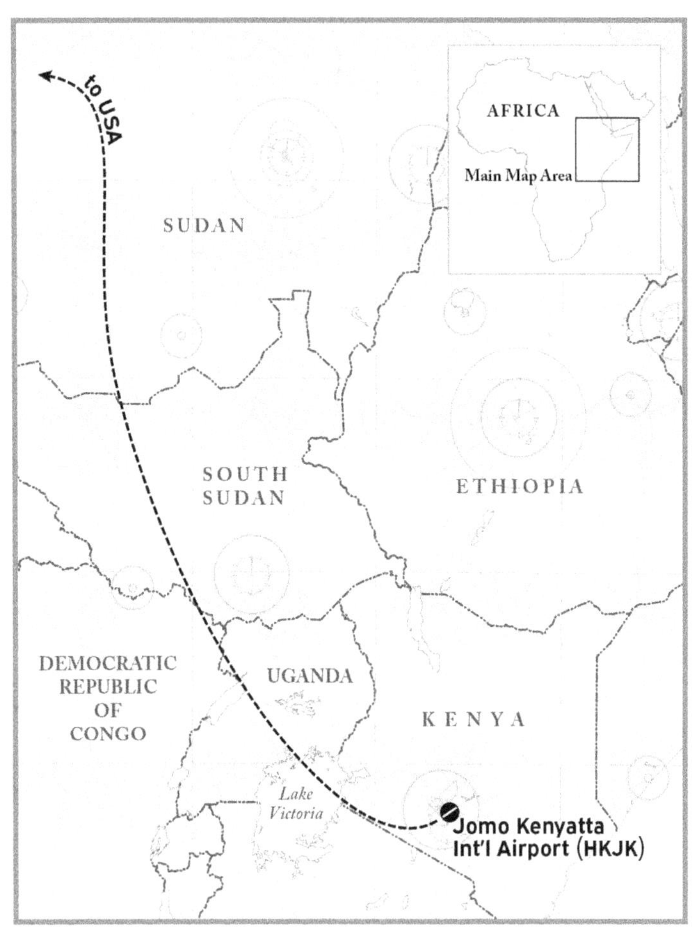
to USA
AFRICA
Main Map Area
SUDAN
SOUTH SUDAN
ETHIOPIA
DEMOCRATIC REPUBLIC OF CONGO
UGANDA
KENYA
Lake Victoria
Jomo Kenyatta Int'l Airport (HKJK)

HOME AGAIN

This, I believe, is the great Western truth: that each of us is a completely unique creature and that, if we are ever to give any gift to the world, it will have to come out of our own experience and fulfillment of our own potentialities, not someone else's.

– Joseph Campbell

During those months in Africa, I had held up my end of the bargain. I did what I could to help, to patch up, to save. We had flown to extraordinary places, and I had worked with talented nurses and pilots. We had visited frontiers in eleven countries, saved a few lives, seen some remarkable clinical cases, and made (mostly) the right calls.

In that journey as an airborne doctor, I had been a witness to some of the extraordinary work the Flying Doctors has done over their sixty years in East Africa. I try to remember how miraculous it must seem, when lying hurt and vulnerable in one of the most hostile and remote places in the world, to see the white silhouette of a Flying Doctor's plane circling the runway. And then to watch as the pilot expertly wedges a plane between trees on a field filled with gazelles and zebras. How miraculous it must seem to experience the ministrations of a doctor and nurse and to feel safe again in the presence of extraordinary competence as the plane takes off toward Nairobi, knowing that the worst is behind you. It must be a humbling, deeply human experience of extraordinary relief.

In that bar in Santa Fe, years earlier, I had told Tom Rees that I wanted to come to Africa to clear my mind and reevaluate my professional goals—to experience simpler, more intimate relationships with my patients, and maybe to figure out how to tolerate a system of industrial medicine. Tom urged me to immerse myself in Africa, to find the path I should be on, to discover my destiny. He had concluded the introductory pages of his autobiography with a similar missive to his readers: "I offer these stories to you, the reader, in the hope that they will inspire in you the courage to seek your own destiny and the desire, as Joseph Campbell has put it, to find your bliss."

I recognized Tom's reference to Joseph Campbell. A renowned scholar of literature, specializing in comparative mythology and religion, Campbell had become a well-known public figure and an unlikely spiritual guru in the 1980s. Years later, after I had reflected on the wisdom of that evening in Santa Fe, I realized that I had missed the crumbs that Tom had left for me in the forest. Campbell's wildly popular PBS interviews with journalist Bill Moyers were published in a book, *The Power of Myth,* and I bought a copy. In the book, Campbell stressed the importance of uncovering the deep mysteries of oneself, of taking a journey inward, of listening for the sounds of transformation, of living to our potential. He would have clearly recognized Dag Hammarskjöld's journeys through Africa—and probably Tom's and mine, as well—for what they were: heroic, faraway travels that brought us closer to ourselves. "Where we had thought to travel outward," Campbell wrote, "we will come to the center of our own existence."

I would have loved to have spoken with Tom Rees once again, to share my adventures and to tell him that I thought that I had finally figured out what he had been saying—that I finally understood my remarkable journey. My needs—and desires— explained why I had so quickly said yes to this beschert, almost preordained work as a Flying Doctor. It would explain how I found the frontiers that Hammarskjöld described as so necessary to understand my identity and talents as a healer. How I, too, had been trained in the African depths.

I never did have that conversation. Tom would die at his home, of liver cancer, a few months after I returned home from Nairobi. He was the last of the Flying Doctors' founding members. Our itineraries had been different, but I suspect that our journeys were similar. Africa's hidden frontiers led us all to recognize in ourselves something which we really knew all the time.

I left Wilson airport, likely for the last time, in 2012. I was newly married, and I would, against all expectations, soon become a father. My essential desire to stay in motion was outweighed by budding responsibilities at home in a way that felt primal and surprising.

In the end, I learned that the world is a complicated place. Professional and societal life are defined by interests and systems and politics and forces beyond ourselves. Africa has its own different and serious problems. But this didn't mean that I should let myself be pulled off-course by quotidian troubles and pedestrian problems, the distractions. There was a world of opportunity to reemphasize the higher purpose of being a healer, to apply my talents to myriad real problems, to try to improve things. I learned I wasn't hostage to my immediate circumstances. I could be an agent in the chaos.

That's how my grand voyage through East Africa ended. I wonder, sometimes, if I really needed to go to Africa to find my frontier. Maybe, if I had been more introspective, or had listened more, my journey might have been less onerous, less far away, less dangerous. Who knows?

I headed home on an airliner with Germans and evangelicals and an extraordinary set of memories that I would share with my future children, maybe in a book when I finally got my thoughts organized. If I wrote that book, I'd probably write as its conclusion that I had left America feeling like my purpose was unclear and returned as a better doctor, far more certain of my path forward as a healer. I would take my children by the hand and show them on the map where I used to fly and tell them that I had thrown myself open, with courage and humility. I had danced at the frontier, and then I had understood. It was an extraordinary journey of self-discovery.

In those precious months, East Africa's hidden places had revealed themselves in unforgettable ways. I'd seen tragedy befall the innocent, and I'd seen miracles happen with stunning regularity. I was witness to unexpected scenes of extraordinary bravery and shameful cowardice. I'd met survivors of dreadful abuse and advocates for those who suffered. I administered to the devout and the hypocritical, to martyrs and to dictators. I met humans who, with profound love and perseverance, committed to raise their children to become honorable adults. I'd experienced winds and rains which grounded planes and left people to die; and tribal rituals of visceral energy which raised the dead. I'd seen children caged, while others were freed by the miracle of modern medicine. Our flights, in sum, through sheer moxie and purpose, became modest entries in AMREF's thick book of legends.

Are those days gone? Have I thoroughly mapped my own frontiers? I don't know. I hope so. The road still beckons. But, for now, I have found my bliss.

EPILOGUE

Is the system going to flatten you out and deny you your humanity, or are you going to be able to make use of the system to the attainment of human purposes?

– Joseph Campbell

Not long after I returned from Africa, I started to dedicate myself to building a better model of health care. Fixing the system from within seemed a Herculean task. I chose instead to work for young, innovative health care companies that would compete with the entrenched incumbents by offering more patient-focused and affordable care. Over the next decade, I helped lead a handful of impactful health care delivery companies in the US and abroad. I was, and remain, driven by a vision of creating human-scale, affordable, rational health care.

AMREF Flying Doctors, too, has continued to thrive. They have added aircraft to their fleet and were the winner of the international air ambulance of the year award twice, beating every other air ambulance service globally. In 2022, the service responded to roughly a thousand emergency calls, nearly three calls every day. Sixty years after being founded by three volunteer surgeons, AMREF is now the largest Africa-based NGO, offering programs in thirty-five countries while managing an annual budget of $221M.

ACKNOWLEDGMENTS

One's path in life often is determined by a few heroic people—extraordinary mentors who are there at just the right time, people who recognize "something" in a newcomer. In my life, so far, there have been eight such people: Lew Evans, Millie Sandleben, Father Doctor, Abby Wolfson, Walt Stoy, Mike Richards, Armin Ernst, and Rushika Fernandopulle. Each arrived in my life at a pivotal time and made all the difference. They recognized my passions, my talents, and my weaknesses; they swatted away bureaucracy and opened doors and created space for me to develop. My being able to write this book, as a doctor and as a world citizen, is a testament to their efforts. Two of these giants have died; the rest, I'm thrilled to still call my friends. Thank you.

As with many things I've attempted, I set off clueless as a novice writer, and I had the great luck to be welcomed into a community of "book people" who nurtured my interest. Larry O'Connor and Sarah Williams read early drafts of this book and gave me great advice. Talented copyeditor Leslie Wilson perfected the text, and Peris Omwoa provided invaluable help as a fact checker. Gordon Rothman guided the audiobook version of *Urgent Calls,* and Elias Othitis and his talented team at e-AudioProductions produced it. Cartographer Elbie Bentley produced the book's gorgeous maps. The book's talented designers, Xavier Comas and Rafa Andres Pio, and their team at Cover Kitchen designed and typeset the book beautifully. Dalyn Miller and Corinne Kalasky promoted it with enthusiasm and engagement.

Finally, my extraordinary editor Katie Hall, who—beyond tearing apart and rebuilding the manuscript multiple times—served as the book's majordomo, main cheerleader, and experienced guide through the publishing wilderness. *Urgent Calls* wouldn't have been completed without her.

My fellow crew members—the dedicated Kenyan nurses and pilots I flew with— performed heroically and kept me safe. They, and my many patients, never failed to teach me something new. Former Flying Doctors Medical Director Dr. Bettina Vadera was an inspiration. More recently, the AMREF Canada and AMREF Nairobi teams have been invaluable. At AMREF Canada, Aisha

Poitevien, Sharon Broughton, Navin Singh, Wanjiru Munene, and Melina Kalamandeen have been engaged and helpful. In Kenya, Country Director Dr. Meshack Ndriangu and Flying Doctors CMO Dr. Joseph Lelo have provided great support. Part of the proceeds of this book will be donated to Flying Doctors to support their charity flight program.

I was fortunate to have the space and encouragement to write and revise this book. My wife, Martina Stippler, and my children, Oscar and Nora, tolerated—without complaint—my many long absences. In recent years, those absences amounted to hundreds of days a year spent abroad so that I could pursue my passions of writing, global health, and travel. Martina makes endless allowances for my atypical schemes, and she carries the load, again and again. Martina: I can't thank you enough.

BIOGRAPHY

Marc-David Munk is an emergency physician and health care executive. Over the past decade, he has held leadership roles at a range of nontraditional health care delivery organizations. Munk began his career as a professor of emergency medicine and as the medical director for the Qatari national ambulance service. He later became a senior executive at high-performing physician groups in the US and abroad. In 2024, he entered a second career as a hospice and palliative care physician.

Munk grew up in Switzerland and Canada. He graduated from Colgate University with a BA in philosophy and religion and completed an MPH in international health from Boston University. After graduating from Philadelphia's Jefferson Medical College, he did residency training in emergency medicine, completed a clinical fellowship in international health at the University of Pittsburgh, and then completed a Diploma in Tropical Medicine and Hygiene at Peru's Gorgas Program. He also holds a master's degree in health care management from Harvard University.

Munk lives outside Boston with his wife and his two children.

Urgent Calls from Distant Places is his first book.

BIBLIOGRAPHY

1. "Body and soul contain a thousand possibilities..." Hammarskjöld, Dag. 1966. *Markings.* London: Faber and Faber.

2. "I sought trains..." Theroux, Paul. 2006. *The Great Railway Bazaar: By Train Through Asia.* Boston: Houghton Mifflin.

3. "We began every morning..." Markham, Beryl. *1987. West with the Night.* New York: Spoken Arts.

4. "Although I had no idea what would come..." Rees, Thomas. 2002. *Daktari: A Surgeon's Adventures with the Flying Doctors of East Africa.* Santa Fe, NM: Sunstone Press.

5. "It might be said that a great unstated reason for travel..." Theroux, Paul. 2011. *The Tao of Travel:*

Enlightenment from Lives on the Road. Boston: Houghton Mifflin Harcourt.

6. "We're governed by our religion…" Al-Bashir, Omar. 2007. "Sudanese President Omar al-Bashir." Interviewed by Ann Curry. NBC News, June 22.

7. "The atheist staring from his attic…" Martin Buber quoted by Garret Barden, S.J. in his introduction to Jean Lacroix's *The Meaning of Modern Atheism* (Macmillan: New York, 1965).

8. "It is not all pleasure this exploration…" Livingstone, David. 2008. *The Last Journals of David Livingstone, in Central Africa, from 1865 to His Death.* Kindle Edition.

9. "Turning and turning in the widening gyre…" Yeats, William Butler. "The Second Coming." *Poetry Foundation.* https://www.poetryfoundation.org/poems/43290/the-second-coming. Accessed November 4, 2023.

10. "To mess around with Ebola is an easy way to die…"

Preston, Richard. 1995. *The Hot Zone.* New York: Anchor Books.

11. "The crowd doesn't have to know…" Attributed to Benito Mussolini, quoted in Albright, Madeleine. 2018. *Fascism: A Warning.*

12. "People think that epilepsy is divine…" Attributed to Hippocrates. https://www.hippocraticfoundation.org.

13. "A Clock stopped…" Dickinson, Emily. "A Clock Stopped-." In Franklin, R. W., ed. 1999. *The Poems of Emily Dickinson.* Cambridge, MA: Belknap Press.

14. "I went through life bada-bing…" Attributed to Evel Knievel.

15. "We are not human beings having a spiritual experience…" De Chardin, Pierre Teilhard. 1959. *The Phenomenon of Man.* New York: Harper.

16. "Sola dosis facit venenum…" Kethna, Hema, ed. 2020. *Toxicology for the Clinical and Forensic Labo-*

ratory. London: Elsevier Academic Press.

17. "The star thrower is a man…" Eiseley, Loren. 1979. *The Star Thrower.* New York: Harcourt.

18. "All journeys have secret destinations…" Buber, Martin. 1988. *Hasidism and Modern Man.* Atlantic Highlands, NJ: Humanities Press International.

19. "Prevented by the duties of life…" Hammarskjöld, Dag. 1966. *Markings.* London: Faber and Faber.

20. "Any 'discovery' we make about ourselves…" Hammarskjöld, Dag. 1966. *Markings.* London: Faber and Faber.

21. "It is not fickle…" Markham, Beryl. 1987. *West with the Night.* New York: Spoken Arts.

22. "And I believe these are the days of lasers in the jungle…" Simon, Paul. 1987. "The Boy in the Bubble." Track 3 on *Graceland.* Warner Bros Records.

23. "Yet may God place a shield of coolest air…" Hasan,

Sayyid Mahammad Abdille. Quoted in Samatar, Said S. 1982. *Oral Poetry and Somali Nationalism: The Case of Sayyid Mahammad Abdille Hasan.* Cambridge: Cambridge University Press.

24. "When the lambs are lost in the mountain…" McCarthy, Cormac. 2001. *Blood Meridian, or, The Evening Redness in the West.* New York: Modern Library.

25. "The air is full of the laughter of machines…" Stanley-Wrench, Margaret. "The New Swallows." *Poetry Foundation.* Accessed November 11, 2023. https://www.poetryfoundation.org/poetrymagazine/browse?contentId=23239.

26. "Schwarze Milch der Frühe…" Celan, Paul. "Todesfuge." *Lyrik line.* Accessed November 11, 2023. https://www.lyrikline.org/de/gedichte/todesfuge-66.

27. "This, I believe, is the great Western truth…" Campbell, Joseph. 1988. *The Power of Myth.* New York: Doubleday.

28. "Is the system going to flatten you out…" Campbell,

Joseph. 1988. *The Power of Myth.* New York: Doubleday.

Milton Keynes UK
Ingram Content Group UK Ltd.
UKHW040146310124
436936UK00017BA/439/J